"Ivan Farber has a reputation for taking on challenges and working diligently and thoughtfully until he masters them. This book is no exception. As a former manager in business now working as a mental health counselor, I would recommend this book to all who want to improve their conversations, relationships, understanding and being understood."

—Margaret Evans MBA, LPC

"Ivan invites the reader to use client facing and client engaging best practices that build trust and connect with clients in an authentic manner using a process that is both repeatable and measurable. In this template driven digital word where so many business books follow the same track, it's absolutely refreshing to get back to tactical ideas that anyone in ANY industry can use day-to-day with clients. Ivan uses real world examples to demonstrate proven ways to connect with clients to understand them and earn their clients most valued asset, their trust."

—Alex Brown, Independent Consultant,
SOAR Performance Group

"Ivan and I worked together during the 1990s when he was beginning his career. He has said that I was a good teacher / mentor to him. However, I learned much from Ivan and still do. He is a great student of life and his enthusiasm and genuine desire to share his stories is a gift. I feel blessed to have worked with Ivan.

I highly recommend reading and rereading Conversations, in order to achieve success in both your personal and professional life. Learn how to have clear conversations with all of the people in your life and live a happy and fulfilled life."

—Catherine Norcott, CFP Certified Financial Planner™,
Realtor®, Private Lender

CONVERSATIONS

▲

How to Manage Your Business Relationships
One Conversation at a Time

Ivan S. Farber

Print Book ISBN-13: 978-1-7321646-5-9
eBook ISBN-13: 978-1-7321646-6-6

Cover design by O'Daniel Designs

Printed by Gorham Printing in the United States of America

Legacy ONE AUTHORS

Kirkland, WA

LegacyOneAuthors.com

TABLE OF CONTENTS

ACKNOWLEDGMENTS

TO MY PARENTS, Ruth and Barry Farber, for loving me so much and for making sure I was provided with a rich and robust education.

To my brother, Paul Farber, for continually inspiring me with his creative and worthy endeavors.

To my cousin, Phyllis Libou, who thoughtfully reads anything and everything I write and always provides me with timely and encouraging feedback.

To my wife, Wendy Farber, for being my life partner and fully supporting and believing in me.

To my close colleagues who have been there to provide significant input, feedback and encouragement for the past several years: Aaron Brown, Janelle Buzzell, Daniel Lovato, Truls Skogsrud and Michael Van Sant. Thank you for believing in my vision and helping me bring it to fruition.

To my writing coach, Karen Lynn Maher, who helped me get unstuck and provided me a process and structure to make the book better, stronger and more impactful.

To all those who've mentored and coached me or given me the opportunity to mentor or coach them.

I am grateful.

AUTHOR'S NOTES

Stories: I tell many stories in the book about conversations with my clients and colleagues throughout the years. To avoid any possibility that someone might be recognizable, I've changed all the names.

Client: I chose to use the word client instead of customer. A client is someone who develops an enduring and valuable relationship with a professional. A customer is someone who purchases products or services from your company, but the relationship is transactional in nature and there isn't necessarily an expectation of it continuing.

Relationship Manager: I selected the term relationship manager because it was generic enough to encapsulate all the different roles where a relationship with a specific person is an important and essential part of a client's relationship with a company. While there are tons of books for salespeople and customer service representatives, there aren't very many for relationship managers—people who are in a hybrid role that is part sales and part service.

Pronouns: I mostly use the male pronouns "he" and "him" throughout the book instead of alternating between "he" and "she." My goal is not to diminish the role women play as relationship managers, but to keep things simpler and also to avoid referring to individuals as "they" or "them."

Application of My Ideas: Although the book is written with business and business people in mind, the processes and ideas discussed in the book can be applied to all your relationships—especially your most important ones. Operating in a needs-based fashion in your conversations enhances your ability to contribute and collaborate with the people in your life. We all have needs and to the degree that we can help other people get what they need, it's much more likely they will help us in return.

PREFACE

WHY IS IT THAT some conversations increase client satisfaction and loyalty while others go nowhere or spin out-of-control? After closely observing 10,000 conversations, I've concluded that the major problem relationship managers have in working effectively with their clients is very few of them have a system, process, method or formula for managing their conversations. They stay too surface level and transactional and as a result don't address their clients' true needs.

The purpose of this book is to teach relationship managers how to successfully manage their client relationships one conversation at a time.

Success in your career depends upon your ability to gain agreement for action. If you improve your ability to retain and grow client relationships through powerful conversations, you'll become more valuable to your company, make more money, and increase your job satisfaction. There is no skill more important than the ability to be effective in conversations.

Early in my career I had reasons, excuses and stories about what my clients did or didn't do. Everything changed the day I realized it was more powerful to hold myself fully accountable for creating my client relationships through the conversations I was having. I decided to be 100% responsible for all results and outcomes and I kept score by looking at the metrics measuring client retention, additional business and referrals.

As I became more and more accomplished in my career, it became clear to me that in addition to the experience of being deeply connected to my clients, the business results at the companies I worked for showed the success of my methods and experiments. As my career has progressed, I've consistently taken on more and more responsibility for larger and more important client relationships. Over the years, I've managed thousands of relationships and won billions in new business. I'm humbled by my success and also proud. I still feel driven every day and work to improve. I know I can still get a lot better.

I believe the lessons I share in this book will make you better at your job, improve your company's bottom line business results, and ultimately make the business world a better place.

INTRODUCTION

WHEN I WAS A CHILD, I saw a psychiatrist every day (my father). I also saw a psychologist every day (my mother). This is significant because although I chose to work in business, my upbringing greatly shaped how I think about business, relationships and conversations. One of the most important things I learned was how to solve problems through conversations. Relationships are made up of many conversations. Just like a chain is only as strong as its weakest link, a relationship is only as strong as its weakest conversation.

After I graduated from college, my mother had a conversation with me to explore my future career goals. She wondered if I might be interested in the mental health field because she knew I wanted to work in a profession where I could help others overcome their fears and work toward fulfillment and self-actualization. Instead of the mental health field, I chose to work in financial services. In many ways it's the business version of the mental health profession because when it comes to money—dealing with it, managing it and making decisions about it—it's highly psychological.

During my 25-year career in the financial services industry, I've had a front row seat to the dot-com bubble inflating and then bursting, a stock market panic and a mortgage meltdown. Each of those experiences involved counseling clients in emotional and pressure-filled situations. While developing conversation management skills for peak emotional events is important, I believe clients also need your advice and counsel in every single interaction. The more you develop your skills, the more you can help your clients make better decisions, find better solutions and ultimately have better lives.

Ten years ago, I decided to approach my conversations scientifically and focus on my process and technique. I invested a lot of effort in determining what worked and what didn't. Due to the sheer number of conversations—

10,000—I was able to test many different conversational concepts. I learned which techniques and strategies were effective while also determining the ones that failed consistently and left both me and my client disempowered. I treated the opportunity to experiment as a conversation laboratory and sought to discover the formula for a highly effective conversation.

Relationships are complex and conversations are the space in which relationships live. At a fundamental level, a conversation is the way we get what we want and need in the world. It's where relationships thrive and prosper or wither and die. Improving business relationships has always fascinated me. Einstein worked his whole life to develop a unified theory on energy and matter and I've worked my whole life to develop a unified theory on conversations and business relationships.

Life is one big experiment. I've experimented a lot and I've made a lot of mistakes—still do. The mistakes in my lab are what have taught me the most. While my mentors, managers and colleagues have mostly provided positive feedback, with some very impactful and sometimes devastatingly constructive feedback along the way, the biggest critic of all was (and continues to be) my internal voice. It constantly drives my improvement.

Some people are naturally good at talking with others while others need to work hard to develop their skills. I'm someone who wasn't necessarily a natural. This means I'm able to teach what I've learned to others because I had to first learn it myself. Over time, I watched myself go from being consciously incompetent to becoming consciously competent of what was I was doing. This contrasts with those who start off unconsciously competent and don't have to figure out what to do at all. They may not even know what strategies they're using to be successful so it makes it hard for them to teach their strategy to others.

Thank you in advance for considering the ideas in this book and joining me in a conversation about conversations. I believe you will find the ideas in this book to be thought-provoking and immediately applicable to your job, your career and your life.

This is a how-to book—it's how to do it like me. But, please know that by no means do I think this the perfect way or the only way. No one has a monopoly on perfect and I surely don't. I still learn from mistakes I make every day.

Lesson 1 • Build Rapport

HAVE YOU EVER FOUND yourself in an awkward or difficult conversation? Of course, if you interact with people, both situations are inevitable. When it's awkward you might think, "I wish we were more at ease." When it's difficult you might think, "Why does this have to be so hard? We're just talking!"

Conversations can be stressful and just getting through them can be a great source of frustration. Maybe you sense the client you're speaking with doesn't like you or trust you. Or, maybe he's resisting where you want to take the conversation. Consider this concept: whenever you or your client are having a negative experience in a conversation, it's a signal that rapport is missing and you need to build it.

Being successful in life, in business and in your relationships requires you to become comfortable in the face of awkward or difficult conversations. The best way for you to become comfortable and put your clients at ease is to master the art of building rapport.

So, what exactly is rapport?

Rapport is a close and harmonious relationship in which the people or groups concerned understand each other's feelings or ideas and communicate well.

Here are a few observations about rapport:

- Rapport happens when you and your client have the experience that you like and trust each other.

- Rapport acts as the context, background and setting for all your relationships.
- Rapport creates comfort. It's like an anti-anxiety medication. When you have rapport with someone you can sit in silence and it doesn't feel awkward, or you can speak freely without a high degree of fear.
- Rapport continuously impacts the effectiveness of every one of your conversations and goes a long way toward determining their outcomes.
- Metaphorically speaking, the rapport in a conversation is like the ambiance in a restaurant. A good ambiance creates a background for an enjoyable meal.

I believe we constantly ask ourselves test questions (consciously or subconsciously) when we interact with someone.

Among those questions are:

1. Does he like me?
2. Does he trust me?
3. Do I like him?
4. Do I trust him?

Here are two thought-provoking questions for you to ask yourself:

1. Whom do you like more: someone whom you trust or someone you distrust?
2. Whom do you trust more: someone whom you like or someone you dislike?

I don't know how you answered the above, but from my perspective, if I don't trust someone, it's hard for me to like him and if I don't like him it's hard for me to trust him. Liking and trusting someone are completely connected, which is why rapport is the foundation for conversation and relationship management.

For some relationship managers, establishing rapport with their clients is easy, and they do it naturally, but for others that's not the case at all—they frequently find themselves having awkward conversations. Many relationship managers don't even know what rapport is or give any conscious thought to it. Or, if they do know what it is, they haven't thought about how to get it when it's not present.

Your effectiveness as a relationship manager depends upon your ability to get your clients to like you and trust you. Therefore, the ability to establish and maintain rapport in a conversation is essential. An added benefit of rapport is that it's much more enjoyable and fun to do business with a client with whom you have rapport.

While the concept of rapport is intangible, most people know whether rapport is present or not. How do they know? Because the experience of a conversation where there's rapport is usually relaxed and flowing. It's easier to collaborate. In contrast, without rapport the experience can be difficult, tense, or antagonistic.

For you to be effective in conversations with your clients, you must develop your skill in building rapport no matter how difficult the circumstances (or people) are. Building rapport is vital to building a relationship.

An Upset Psychoanalyst

I sat down on the psychoanalyst's couch, but I wasn't there to tell her my problems—just the contrary. Mary had been with our company for well over a decade and I was her brand-new relationship manager. She was unhappy about being assigned a new relationship manager and there I was, in her living room, introducing myself.

Mary started off by telling me how upset she was. She shared many concerns with me and although I knew better, I started by responding to each one logically and systematically. With each response, I could see her growing more and more upset. Our conversation wasn't going well. Management had given me the responsibility for this very important relationship and I couldn't help but think I may have been dealt a bad hand.

Luckily, I decided to change my approach before things went too far awry. I let her know I'd fully address everything she'd brought up, but before doing so, I asked if it would be okay to take a little time to get to know her first. Her demeanor and tone changed immediately. She asked what I wanted to know about her. I told her I was interested in learning about how she came to be a psychoanalyst, her family and her upbringing. She proceeded to share important details about her life, her philosophy and her belief system. I listened to her for the next 45 minutes. I accomplished much more by listening than talking. She said she felt much better and really appreciated how well I listened to her. When a psychoanalyst tells you that you listen well, it's a high compliment. I thanked her for sharing about herself. Asking about her life worked to change the entire dynamic of the conversation.

The lesson here is to make sure you establish rapport before transacting business. In every conversation, and in every part of a conversation, rapport needs to be present for you to be effective. When a conversation isn't going well it's a clear sign that rapport is missing, and you need to establish or reestablish it. Rapport isn't always going to be easy to establish. Sometimes you'll ask someone to tell you about himself and he'll hardly have anything to say. Because that situation can be awkward, you may have to do some homework and come up with a plan prior to the conversation. In my situation, I knew a lot about the client from her previous relationship manager, but I hadn't heard it from her first hand and she responded well to my curiosity. Listening demonstrated I cared and created a foundation for trust.

Systematically Gather Information

The ability to discover your client's life circumstances beyond the information you need to perform your business functions creates a foundation for a long-term relationship. By showing an interest, it helps your clients know you care about more than just their business. Dale Carnegie said, *"You can make more friends in two months by becoming interested in other people than you can in two years by trying to get other people interested in you."*

Relationship managers typically think achieving rapport means finding things in common, being good at making small talk and telling others about themselves. But it's more than that. In addition to looking for things you have in common, your sincere curiosity also shows respect. When you ask a client to open up and share about himself, treat that as honorably and respectfully as if you were entering his house and offered the opportunity to sit down with him in his living room. When you show interest and excitement (or even fascination) about getting to know a client, it goes a long way.

I first learned about the importance of systematically obtaining information from a book called *Swim With The Sharks...Without Being Eaten Alive* by Harvey Mackay. Mackay was a salesman for an envelope company. And, even though his product was rather simple—envelopes—he found he outsold his competition because he knew his customers better than anyone else. He developed of a list of 66 things he thought he should know about everyone. His list included lots of detailed information about his customers and his relationship with them. Mackay believed that by gathering this information, his customers would feel known and therefore be loyal and purchase exclusively from him.

While there are lots of things you'll get to know about your clients over time, I believe there are four main areas to start with. They are: education, career, family and hobbies/interests.

1. Education

When asking about a client's educational background, I found asking questions such as "Where did you go to college?" to be presumptuous and risky because not everyone went to college. Maybe he went to a vocational school, never finished high school or served in the military. A client who was educated in a foreign country often had a different word than college. Therefore, what I found was a better and safer way to ask about education was simply, "What's your educational background?" It's a simple open-ended question that's not at all threatening. Everyone got educated somehow—even if it was in the school of hard knocks. A client's educational experience is important because it's where a good portion of his world view comes from. Assuming you know what his job is, an additional way to learn about his educational history is to ask how his education played a role in his chosen career and how he got started.

2. Career

Getting a basic overview of a client's career is useful in numerous ways. His perspective on the products or services you offer to him is shaped by the role he's played in his career. Was he the buyer or the seller? Was he a manager, line worker, individual contributor or a lower level associate? How he interacts with you is likely to be very similar to how he interacted with people at work. (For example, if he was a manager, he may speak to you like you are one of his direct reports.)

I prefer to use simple statements such as, "Tell me about your career." or "I'd like to know more about your background." If I know his current job, I'll probably ask, "How did you come to work in your current job as a _____?" Or, when someone is retired I'll ask, "What was your career like?" Followed with, "How did you get started in it?" Sometimes a client will provide you with a short answer but other times he will elaborate. Encouraging him to elaborate is important. Especially in a new relationship, giving a client the opportunity to tell you about himself helps him to feel understood and begins to build a base of trust. Sometimes a client won't want to share very much at all—he'll give you very short answers and hold his cards close to his chest. It's easy to assume he won't ever open up, but don't. You just need to find a topic he likes to talk about. Be thoughtful and creative. Try to put yourself in his shoes.

3. Family

Understanding a client's family situation also tells you a lot about his experience in the world. To get him to open up without appearing too intrusive, it pays to start with questions that are easy to answer like: "Where did you grow up?" or "Where does most of your family live?" or "How many siblings do you have?" Getting your client's marital status can sometimes be awkward. Asking a client, "Are you married?" may occur as nosy or too direct. A generic request like: "Please tell me about your family situation" gives him the choice of what he wants to share. It's the same thing with children: "Do you have any children?" could be perceived as somewhat of an odd question. He might think (or say), "What does that have to do with me buying your services?" Notwithstanding, if you're going to claim you got to know someone and didn't ask about his family situation, you're missing a big part of his world.

4. Hobbies/Interests

Asking your client about his hobbies or interests can sometimes help get them to open up, but it can also land flat with a client who doesn't have what he would consider to be a hobby. Perhaps he's someone who works all the time. Questions such as "What do you like to do for fun?" or "What do you do when you're not working?" can also land flat. So, over time, as I've experimented with different questions, I've found, "What are your hobbies and interests?" is the simplest and broadest way to start. Saying what you like to do first can work too. I'll say, "So, I like to exercise and spend time with my family, what about you?" Prefacing what could be considered an invasive question by volunteering something about yourself first makes it safer for him to share in return.

Gathering information in all 4 of these areas is essential if you're going to build rapport and have a good sense of who your client is. For many clients, the effect of simply being asked questions about these four major topics gives them the feeling you're sincerely interested and care about them personally and not just with getting and/or keeping their business. This also provides you with a systematic plan for handling the occasional awkward conversation of getting to know someone. While finding commonalities with your clients is a part of generating rapport, there's much more to it.

Make a Rapport Sandwich

A rapport sandwich is made by wrapping a parting comment at the end of a conversation that relates to something said in the beginning. It reaffirms to your client that you were listening and that an important connection was made at the beginning of and during the conversation. It ties the entire conversation together nicely like the top slice of bread completes a sandwich.

When I started in the business world, I was so serious and objective-oriented I didn't realize the value of taking time to relate to people first. My mentor, Julie, emphasized the importance of getting a conversation started on a friendly note. Julie pointed out I failed to start conversations off with a friendly greeting. She suggested that I say something simple like, "Hello, how are you?" which is how we normally greet people in the world. But like a lot of young professionally-inclined men, I was so focused on business that I forgot to be people-focused first. After thousands of conversations, I learned not only to greet people warmly but also how valuable it is to ask a second and third rapport question. This is because the answer to the question, "How are you?" is typically only a one-word answer. And, while it's true that "How are you?" followed by "Fine," is a friendly dance of a greeting, it doesn't really tell you much and doesn't get the other person talking. You'll most likely get conventional answers like: good, well or not too bad.

Asking a second and third rapport question is designed to get the person talking and draw them out. It gives you more meat for your rapport sandwich and helps develop the experience of relatedness. Going beyond "How are you?" works to create flow and ease at the start of a conversation. Curiosity got a bad name when it got blamed for killing the cat. In fact, it's essential to good communication. Becoming comfortable and even excited by your curiosity will open doors.

One of my favorite questions to get into someone else's world is just that: "What's going on in your world?" It's a little bit different than "How are you?" and something you don't hear every day and causes people to think more globally instead of narrowly about their answer.

You can (and need to) go beyond the first open-ended question of "How are you?" if you're going to make any headway and become more than just superficially connected with your client. I like to follow up with another open-ended question: "What's new?" or "What's going on in your neck of the woods?" or "What are your plans for the spring/summer/fall/winter?"

I've also found while the answer to the first question is typically a reflexive dud, the answer to the second question can also fail to get people going. But, upon being asked a third open-ended question in a row, I find people will start to open up. I think asking a third question indicates your sincere interest in them. It's easy to stop at one or two and that's what most people do. The third question noted below is what starts the process of making a rapport sandwich.

1. The question "How are you?" can be limiting. Since it can be answered with one word, "Fine," it doesn't open the door to learning more about your client.

2. This is also true of questions like "What's new?" which can also be answered with one comment, "Nothing much." This closes the door on more questions.

3. However, a question like, "How's your family doing?" increases the likelihood he'll provide more information. It's easier for him to volunteer information about others.

If you can't think of anything to ask and you're looking for a fail-safe question for anyone, anyplace or anytime, you can ask about the weather. We all have weather in common and it's hard to resist a super easy question like: "What do you think about the weather?" Asking about the weather is a great icebreaker and conversation starter—perhaps the best because it's so easy (and safe) for people to answer. At the same time, someone who's more business-focused, might appreciate "How's business?" or "What have you been working on lately?"

In addition to spending the first few minutes of every conversation asking a second or third rapport question, I'll finish the rapport sandwich at the end of a conversation with a farewell comment tied to something I learned at the beginning of the conversation. If I learned he was going on a safari in West Africa, I wish him a good trip. If he told me he was painting his kitchen, I wish him enjoyment on painting his kitchen. As I mentioned early in the chapter, tying your parting comment to something from the beginning of the conversation is what makes it a rapport sandwich and will leave your client feeling as though you were really listening to him throughout the conversation.

As we move on to learning about other strategies for establishing rapport, I want to emphasize that rapport isn't just talking about what you have in common or talking about personal things in addition to business topics—it's much more.

Match Non-Verbal Communication

Since only a small part of our communication is verbal, a lot of rapport comes from our body language, vocal quality and tone. Matching your client's non-verbal communication is a valid strategy for building rapport. When you're matching your client, it can mean you sit like he sits, hold your posture like he holds his posture or look where he's looking. You don't have to (and really shouldn't) match him exactly as he may notice it or feel like you're mocking him. Matching one item is enough. He crosses his legs, you cross your legs. He crosses his arms, you cross your arms. He leans to one side, you lean to one side.

Some say matching intentionally is unnatural and manipulative, but anytime you are in rapport with your client, by definition, you're, in fact, matching him in some way. So, why not intentionally match your client to help him feel more comfortable with you? Having him feel comfortable is one of your goals. If your non-verbal communication is discordant or incongruous, you undermine rapport.

Matching non-verbal communication can also help you to empathize with your client. When you match someone's body positioning you're able to get a sense for how he feels. You can experience this in your own conversation lab. In your next conversation with a client, hold the same posture as his and check to see if that helps you relate to him.

Can matching non-verbal communication be done over the phone when you can't see the other person? My answer is yes, absolutely. Although I don't have any conclusive evidence of this, my intuition tells me that if you've achieved deep rapport with your client, your body language on one side of the phone conversation is likely matched on the other. Other non-verbal elements you can match over the phone are your client's vocal qualities: their tone, pace and pitch. Moreover, the ultimate rapport builder, is laughter. Laughter brings people closer together. It gives you instant commonality. It makes you likeable and real. It could be a result of a joke, a story, an unexpected outcome or the laughter of recognition when a hidden truth is named.

There are three major sensory perception qualities that people use when they communicate. They are: visual, auditory and kinesthetic (seeing, hearing and feeling). You can easily and quickly observe them in how people talk:

Visual Statements:

"This is how it looks to me."
"I just can't picture myself doing that."
"Do you see what I mean?"
"Look at it this way…"

Auditory/Hearing Statements:

"It sounds good to me."
"That doesn't ring a bell."
"Do you hear what I'm saying?"
"Listen…"

Kinesthetic/Feeling/Physical Statements:

"It doesn't feel right."
"I'm just not in touch with things."
"I sense a good vibe."
"I need to get my ducks in a row."

In conversations, it pays to match your client's descriptive words and basic representations. For example, in talking about stocks with a visually oriented client: "Over time you'll see a long-term uptrend"; with an auditorily oriented client: "We've all heard of the long-term uptrend"; and with a kinesthetically oriented person: "Over time, one holds on to the idea of a long uptrend…"

Find your client's style by paying attention to the words he uses to describe things and then match him. For example, if he says, "Do you see what I mean?" answer "Yes, I see what you mean." Notice how it would sound if you were to respond to "Do you see what I mean?" with "I hear what you mean," or "I feel what you mean."

Experiment with this in your own conversations, but in my experience, matching words increases the level of rapport. Trust and affinity are increased because I am describing the world in a similar way.

Support and Adapt to Style Preferences

Thinking vs. Feeling Orientation

Another style preference to observe is a tendency toward thinking or feeling. You can learn your client's primary style by stating an opinion and following it up with a thinking/feeling double question. "Stocks are going to have a good year. What do you think? How do you feel?" In general, I coach against the use of double questions (or back-to-back multiple questions), but this intentional double question helps you to easily determine your client's orientation because if he's a thinker he'll tell you what he thinks and if he's a feeler he'll tell you how he feels.

This is not to say a client who first answers with, "I think ____" is always a thinker or a client who first answers, "I feel ____" is always a feeler. But in the spirit of matching and speaking, if he says "think" then we can start the discussion with why he thinks that way. If he says "feel" then I'll ask, "Why do you feel that way?" Using the same words (and verbs) increases rapport. When you're aligning with his language, he may subconsciously (or consciously) feel closer to you or think/feel he's more in agreement with you.

Internal vs. External

When you need to provide information to your clients, it's important to support the style in which they process information.

For example, some of your clients will process information externally. They need to talk it through with someone else. Other clients process information internally. They need quiet, stillness or time alone.

To bolster rapport, give a client who is an external processor time to talk and encourage him by asking questions. With a client who is an internal processor, you must provide enough time for him to process and respond. If you don't allow sufficient time for an internal processor to process internally, you will disrupt him, undermine rapport and likely frustrate him.

In addition, discover and adapt to his frame of reference. A client who orients to an external frame of reference will look to others (friends, relatives, media, experts and hopefully you) to validate how they think or feel. A client with an internal frame of reference will decide to do things without (and independent of) checking with others (and probably you). In fact, he may discount others' opinions, and simply check with himself. He doesn't form his opinions based on what others do. Others' opinions usually fail to influence him over his own. He is someone who will have to think something is his idea if he is going to do it.

You can learn a client's frame of reference by asking him how he likes to make decisions or by asking how he's made decisions in the past.

Note that matching verbal communication is not the same as agreeing with your client's opinions. Matching verbal communication is a rapport building tool. If you pay attention to all the ways you can match your client verbally and nonverbally you have a treasure trove of tools to establish, build and maintain rapport.

Dealing with an Angry Doctor

Every time my mentee, John, had to deal with a certain doctor, he shuddered. The doctor's last name was Kyle, (but he pronounced it kill, Dr. Kill). There are people in the world who for whatever reason don't realize how their angry demeanor affects others. It's possible Dr. Kyle meant ill will, but it's also possible he just didn't know how he came across. John wished he wasn't so scared of dealing with him. We supposed Dr. Kyle's bedside manner may have been different with his patients, but to John, it was very difficult working with him. Due to how Dr. Kyle made John feel, he did everything he could to avoid interacting with him. Notwithstanding, John felt obligated to fulfill his basic responsibilities and meet the minimum expectations for client interaction. One situation that was particularly challenging for John was when the doctor's check was sent to the wrong address and John was going to have to deliver the bad news.

I suggested that rather than start with the bad news, he could say he was calling for an operational reason, but not say immediately what it was. I noted when you need to deliver bad news it helps to telegraph that you're going to do so. I also reminded him that establishing rapport before dealing with business goes a long way. He was stumped and asked, "How can I get rapport with this guy? He's so angry and stern." I taught my mentee the skill of matching. "If the doctor says two words, you match him with two words. If the doctor uses a gruff tone, you add a little gruffness to your tone." He said, "Won't that make him mad?" I replied, "You would think so, but I've learned through experimentation that adopting the tone and emotional quality of the other person creates a situation where you experience the world similarly to them and vice versa. Empathy is putting yourself in their shoes. Think for a minute what might have caused him to adopt his demeanor. It could be he's faced many hardships. It could be his father beat him. It could be anything. Put yourself in his shoes and don't make how he treats you about you. It probably has nothing to do with you."

My mentee called the doctor and did as I suggested. He matched his tone, pace and manner. After the call he said he felt empowered. He said he felt the power of being terse and gruff, the power of having a rapport plan, and the power of getting on the phone with someone who he'd previously feared and now knew how to handle. The doctor seemed pleased as well. He'd always wondered why John was so afraid of him.

The lesson here is by establishing rapport first, it will make everything easier. Rapport is much more than having things in common. It could simply be using similar words or expressing yourself in similar ways. It's about finding a way to put yourself on the same side of the table. It allows you to relate to your client's experience before transacting business.

Go into a conversation with a clear plan for getting rapport—especially with people you would consider difficult to interact with. It's a surefire way to make your life and your conversations easier.

Conclusion

Consider rapport as the starting point for all your conversations and treat it with as much importance as the topic of the conversation itself. When you've established rapport with your client you'll find things are easier for you. When rapport with your client goes out everything becomes more difficult. Keep rapport in mind throughout a conversation and you'll create a background for relatedness and effectiveness.

Carl Jung said, *"The meeting of two personalities is like the contact of two chemical substances: if there is a reaction, both are transformed."* The transformation could be positive or it could be negative. There are several different expressions we use to describe the experience of talking with someone:

- "We didn't gel with each other."
- "We were like oil and water."
- "He rubbed me the wrong way."

When you establish mutual affinity and trust, the descriptions are the opposite. For example:

- "We looked at it the same way."
- "We clicked."
- "We were on the same page."
- "We were playing from the same sheet of music."

Lest you think you have nothing in common and cannot build rapport with your client, the lesson from this chapter is that everyone has communication preferences that you can match. His preferences, body language and word choices are like a map to communicating with him. You have an abundance of choices to build rapport. If you show interest, gather information, make a rapport sandwich, and match or adapt to non-verbal and verbal communication styles and preferences, you'll be able to build rapport no matter what the circumstances.

Lesson 2 • Use Questions Skillfully

HOW DO YOU FEEL about asking questions? Do you like asking questions or do you prefer to be the one answering them?

I remember leading one training session where I encouraged the participants to ask many more questions than they were currently asking and I encountered significant resistance. One person asked doubtfully, "Can I really ask that many questions? Can I really start the conversation with questions?" He feared asking a lot of questions would make him look pushy, nosy or even rude. He continued, "Isn't it more important to say the right thing instead of asking questions?" Ironically, he was asking questions of me. It was the moment when I realized that questions are actually statements—they are an attempt to guide a conversation. Eureka! Questions guide conversations.

Early in my career, I had consistently been told I wasn't asking enough questions, but when I tried to ask more questions I wasn't sure what to ask. I also felt like I was giving up control of the conversation by letting the client talk. Moreover, when I'd get a negative outcome from a question, it made me gun-shy to ask more of them. Like a lot of people, I thought it was better to focus on what I was going to say in the conversation. Everything changed once I developed the ability to ask questions skillfully.

When you don't have the knowledge of how to ask questions skillfully, it's easier and more comfortable to talk and hope the conversation goes in the right direction, but if you're going to manage a conversation, you have to become committed to and good at asking questions. As a matter of practice, I typically start a conversation by making a short statement followed by asking questions.

When I look back, it's kind of a surprising to me that I resisted asking questions, because growing up with parents who were mental health professionals, I learned that asking questions was a productive and positive way to empathize, solve problems and show you care. Of course, the tone and demeanor of the question being asked is very important. The same question can be asked because you're curious or because you don't agree with what's happening.

For example, my grandmother (may she rest in peace) would often say, "Whaddya mean?" While "What do you mean?" is one of the most useful questions you can ask, when she said it she wasn't actually asking for clarity, she was telling you she didn't agree with you. For instance, when I told her I was moving across country, she exclaimed, "Whaddya mean?" The message behind the question was: "No! Why would you do that? I don't want you to do that."

Despite the hang-ups I had with asking questions, I continued to experiment and learned how to use questions skillfully to guide a conversation from start to finish. With questions, my conversations became much more collaborative. I also stopped operating on incorrect assumptions. I became 100% clear that in order to become powerful in my conversations, I had to learn to use questions skillfully.

Use Questions as Tools

While it's commonly believed that the results of conversations are driven by what you say in them, I found that wasn't necessarily the case. What seemed to actually matter more, was what my client said in response to my questions. His answers were driving the results.

Metaphorically speaking, questions are the Swiss army knives of conversations. They can be used to accomplish multiple objectives:

- Start or end a conversation
- Obtain important information (facts, feelings and motivations)
- Clarify needs
- Confirm an understanding
- Engage your client in a dialogue

- Show a sincere interest in your client
- Make a point
- Provoke thoughts or feelings
- Connect with your client and relate to and learn about his experiences
- Open your client's mind to a world of information and ideas

- Direct and guide the action in a conversation
- Allow you to interrupt your client politely
- Be consultative
- Direct the focus of the conversation
- Provide a useful distraction
- Keep your client talking—something that will help you to listen better

Despite the powerful benefits and utility of using questions, most relationship managers don't ask them with confidence or intentionally use them as conversational tools. Relationship managers wind up talking about their company's products and services rather than asking questions and listening to their clients talk about their needs, their experiences and their lives.

Be Intentional About the Type of Question You Ask

The game changer for me happened when I determined the best uses of the two major question types: open-ended questions and closed-ended questions. They are as different as opening or closing a window.

1. Open-ended questions typically start with who, what, when, where, why and how?

2. Closed-ended questions typically start with something like: did you, are you, do you, can you, would you, could you, might you or have you?

The difference in the response you create is noteworthy:

- An open-ended question invites or requests a client to explain his thoughts, feelings or circumstances

- A closed-ended question seeks a yes, no or short answer. The client might provide additional information, but the question doesn't encourage it.

For example, the question, "Where are you from?" wants the same information but gets a very different answer than, "Are you from around here?" The first question gets the name of the place your client is from whereas the second gets a yes or a no.

Through observation and practice, I discovered how each type of question is best used. Knowing how you can use each type of question helps to ensure you use the right one at the right time.

Open-ended questions:

- Generate dialogue
- Direct the conversation and forward the action
- Elicit facts, feelings, motivations, needs and wants
- Help foster learning and understanding

Closed-ended questions:

- Request a quick answer
- Check for acceptance of what you've put forward
- Determine if you've obtained agreement
- Make a statement or point
- Typically cause you to lose the ability to direct the conversation

Let me further demonstrate the difference with a series of three questions asking someone how he feels about his job:

Closed-ended (answered with a yes, no or short answer):

- Do you enjoy your job?
- Do you like your company?
- Is there anything you would change about your career?

Open-ended (answered with something besides yes or no):

- What do you enjoy about your job?
- What do you like about your company?
- What would you want to change about your career?

As you can see with these short examples, the closed-ended questions are less likely to foster dialogue: "Yes, I enjoy my job. Yes, I consider myself successful. Sure, there are things I would change."

The answers to the open-ended questions might be:

- I enjoy my colleagues and my clients.
- I enjoy the challenge of providing advice and counsel.
- I would rate myself as very successful.

The answers to the open-ended questions actually create more questions:

- Who are your colleagues?
- What happens in your conversations?
- How much time do you spend with each client?"

The answers to the closed-ended questions would be more valuable if followed up with an open-ended one. If someone says, "Yes, I enjoy my job." the natural next question would be, "What do you enjoy about your job?" Over time, I learned to skip that first question and simply jump to the second. This allows me to gather information and makes the conversation flow better. If you want depth, you must ask open-ended questions.

I'm suggesting an open-ended question is like opening a window because it facilitates the richness and ease of a dialogue. It's much harder to talk with someone through a closed window. Open-ended questions create an exchange and a dialogue.

By way of review, when I want to generate dialogue, direct the conversation, forward the action, or elicit information, I use an open-ended question. When I want to get a quick and short response, check for acceptance or make a statement or a point, I use a closed-ended one.

I've also observed consistently that people tend to use closed-ended questions much more frequently than open-ended ones. It's especially true of a rookie relationship manager. When he goes to ask a question—because it's what I suggested—it comes out as a closed-ended one. If you pay attention, you'll hear an abundance of closed-ended questions in your conversations. Knowing that questions are an essential part of a nutritious conversation, we must actively choose to use the right type in the right situation.

Open-ended Question Rodeo

One of my mentees, James, had a particularly tough time remembering to ask open-ended questions. In conversations with clients, James constantly asked questions starting with: did you, are you, do you, have you?

As a result, his conversations were awkward and constantly stalled. He lacked the self-awareness to see what he was saying and I kept pounding the table, "You have to use open-ended questions." I strongly encouraged him to start his questions with who, what, when, why or how. Moreover, when I listened to his conversations, I kept track of closed-ended and open-ended questions on a ledger to show him the ratio. The ratio was usually infinite because he simply wasn't using any open-ended ones. His conversations were unnecessarily short. His client's responses in turn were brief. He failed to maintain control and he wasn't able to probe the client's thoughts or feelings at any significant level of depth. Any information he got from a client was because the client thought he needed to share it with him, not because James sought it out.

I took my mentee into a conference room and said, "Look, we're going to play a game. It's called the open-ended question rodeo. I'm going to play the client in a mock scenario and the only way you can respond is with a short open-ended question." I handed him a list of the questions and we started to play. In professional bull riding, a rider needs to stay on the bull for eight seconds, or he fails to receive any score. In my open-ended question rodeo, although it's not easy (neither is staying on a bull for eight seconds) the target was five open-ended questions. It drove home the point that you can continue to ask questions much longer than you would normally feel comfortable with.

Mock scenario one:

Ivan (as client): "I'm afraid the stock market is going to crash."

James (as relationship manager): "Why do you say that?" [open-ended #1]

Ivan: "It's been going up for so long."

James: "How does that make you feel?" [open-ended #2]

Ivan: "Nervous, do you think I should cash out?"

James: "No, we think you should stay the course." [He failed to ask a third open-ended question—no score on the bull ride this time.]

We reversed roles:

Mock scenario two:

James: "I'm afraid the stock market is going to crash."

Ivan: "What's the reason you're bringing that up?" [open-ended #1]

James: "It's been going up for so long."

Ivan: "What do you mean?" [open-ended #2]

James: "Well the market is at an all-time high and the last time it reached new highs it crashed."

Ivan: "What do you think caused it to fall?" [open-ended #3]

James: "I don't know what caused it."

Ivan: "What are your long-term investment objectives?" [open-ended #4] [I resisted asking a closed-ended question such as "Would you like to know what we think?" Instead going in a completely different direction, intentionally.]

James: "What does that have to do with the market?"

Ivan: "Everything. Why do you think I'm asking?" [open-ended #5]

James: "I should focus on my long-term objectives versus the problems of the day?"

Ivan: "Yes, you are correct."

I got to five open-ended questions and then the client made the point for me.

The takeaway for you is to mindfully choose your question type. Most people need to increase the number of open-ended questions; although it doesn't necessarily mean asking five in a row. That's simply to make the point that you can use them much more than might feel natural.

My advice is this: if needed, arm yourself with a list of short open-ended questions until you're able to ask them consistently and semi-automatically. Play the open-ended question rodeo with a colleague or a mentor. The best way to make sure you're going to ask an open-ended question is to start with "what" or "how." Moreover, if you find you've started a question with "do you?" or "are you?" you can even stop yourself mid-question and start over.

Speaking of a list of short open-ended questions, here's the list I handed to my mentee:

- What do you think?
- How do you feel?
- Why?
- What's your opinion?
- What makes you say that?
- How can that be?
- Tell me more.
- Why do you think that?
- What do you mean by that?
- Why do you feel that way?
- For example?
- How come?

- How so?
- How does that affect you?
- What's the impact of that?
- Really?
- Oh?
- Interesting…
- What's changed?
- What's your plan?
- What are your main goals?
- What are your major concerns?

We played the open-ended question rodeo several more times. The practice we did helped him manage his client conversations. He saw positive results immediately. One of the benefits he experienced was he didn't have to work so hard to come up with a question to ask. His clients responded by warming up to him and wound up sharing much more. It helped him to build rapport.

What causes people to use closed-ended questions so prolifically and seemingly instinctively? I don't know. Perhaps they're attached to certain answers and think they can more quickly find them with closed-ended questions. What I do know is once I convince someone I'm coaching to start using open-ended questions, his results improve immediately.

Respond to Questions with Questions

I had a mentee named David who was not comfortable answering questions. One time, I was listening to one of his conversations with a client who asked a question that sounded like an objection. There was a long awkward silence following the client's question. The client sounded skeptical and disgruntled when he voiced his question/objection, "Why don't you have any small cap companies in your portfolio?"

David looked like a deer caught in headlights. He didn't know how to respond. His inclination was to become defensive which is typical of someone receiving an objection. (Many "why" questions are viewed as attacks.) And when someone becomes defensive (because he feels attacked), he generally starts talking to defend or fight and unfortunately doesn't think about where his answer will take the conversation. He forgets to use questions to guide it.

Because it was a phone conversation, the client couldn't see me pass David a note. I wrote: "Ask him: how do you define small cap?" David asked the question somewhat tentatively, but it had the immediate effect that I thought it would. The client sputtered in his response. While one could have presumed he knew what he was asking about, he actually didn't. He couldn't even define the term, admitting he didn't really know. A moment earlier he sounded like an authority who caught David with an objection he couldn't answer and now his objection completely went away. It went on to become a highly productive conversation.

My advice is to avoid answering questions reflexively like what happens to your leg when the doctor hits your knee with a reflex hammer. Clarify most questions with short open-ended questions. Answering questions with a question helps you in four ways:

1.   It buys you time to consider the best way to address your client's question.

2.   It clarifies what the question is trying to communicate.

3.   It helps you begin to figure out the need behind the question.

4.   It allows you to potentially reframe the purpose of the question while also maintaining control of the conversation.

Note: you're not avoiding the question, you will eventually answer his question, but your answer will be much more likely to meet his needs because you'll better understand the question and his needs. One short open-ended question can completely shift the conversation—even and especially when your client is emotional.

Respond to Emotions with Questions

Another important use of questions is in situations where emotions are running high or where someone is verbally attacking you. Your client is upset, and he may have entered the conversation in an aggressive fashion. He may also be in a hurry. A rushed conversation is prone to poor outcomes. When a client is irrational or rushing, he's unlikely to accept a rational explanation.

I'll never forget one urologist, Dr. Peters, who was pissed off because he didn't receive his check by when he thought he was supposed to. He started yelling at me. I can't remember whether he used expletives or not, but it didn't matter whether there was foul language, the aggressiveness was overwhelming.

I've found one of the challenges of working with doctors is they tend to be very short on time and are frequently running late. This forces conversations into very small windows. But, a meaningful, thorough and complete conversation about your finances can't be forced into a five-minute time slot like seeing your doctor can.

Unfortunately, we did actually mess up. Although, I started my response with, "We apologize," Dr. Peters didn't even let me finish. "I need to speak with a manager," he demanded. I looked around for a manager and couldn't locate one. It seems to always work that way. Most of the time I have very little need for a manager, but at that specific point in time, one was nowhere to be found. So, I had to tell the doctor that there wasn't a manager available right now, but that as soon as there was one, I would have them call. He barked, "When will that be?" It was an impossible question for me to answer since I didn't know when I would find one and how soon they would have time in their schedule to call him. I fumbled for an answer and simply told him I would do the best I could. He snarled, "Your best hasn't been very good at all," and he hung up.

When I did finally track down a manager, he called Dr. Peters and asked him one open-ended question, "What happened?" He let him vent and then worked to provide a solution to mollify the client.

This taught me a lesson that when someone is emotional and verbally attacking you, giving an apology or saying, "I understand" before you actually understand or even know what you're apologizing for will just make the client more upset. Ask about their expectations. Dr. Peters said he didn't receive his check when he thought he would, but I never even asked when he thought he was supposed to receive it or if he made that clear when he requested it in the first place. I also didn't ask about the implications of not getting it when he thought he would. I apologized prematurely and that made him even angrier.

Just because your client is rushed doesn't mean you can't (and shouldn't) slow things down by asking a couple of questions. You have to gather information if you're going to effectively help him.

Question Asking Principles

There are four key things you can do to increase your effectiveness in asking questions:

1. Ask one question at a time

Many good questions are poorly executed. A relationship manager may unintentionally ask a run-on question (a series of questions in one question) because he hasn't thought through what he's asking and he's thinking out loud. If you do, your client will be confused. While he may have some idea of the direction you're headed, you're demonstrating a lack of preparation and discipline. They're thinking: "Which question am I supposed to answer? What does my relationship manager really want to know? Do I answer the first question, or the last, or none of them, or just try to answer what I think he wants to hear?" There are exceptions to asking more than one question at a time, but doing it intentionally is different than doing it by accident.

2. Make it clear that you're asking a question

What a lot of people do is try to ask a question without really forming the question as a question. For example, "I don't know if you've read our latest newsletter…" could be viewed as a question—or simply an I don't know statement. But if the relationship manager really wants to know if his customer read it, he could simply ask: "Have you read our latest newsletter?" or "How much time, if any, have you spent reading our latest newsletter?"

3. Ask your question in a concise manner

Short questions are more effective. Writing out your questions ahead of time will help you to edit yourself in advance and be more concise. Write out a draft of your question and then boil it down from there. Clear questions lead to clear responses. As a general rule, three to seven word questions are best.

4. Provide time for an answer

When you're asking a question, but don't wait for an answer, you miss an opportunity. What was the point of asking the question in the first place? A focused and disciplined relationship manager will ask a question and then wait. He will allow the client the opportunity and time to formulate an answer. It might seem awkward to wait, but waiting is key.

Combine Question Types in a Sequence

Just because I advocate for relationship managers to ask many more open-ended questions than they habitually do, it doesn't mean open-ended questions are necessarily better than closed-ended questions. In football, it's often said that a good running game sets up the passing game. In a conversation, a foundation of open-ended questions creates an open dialogue and sets you up for the successful use of closed-ended questions. It's the combination and sequence of open-ended and closed-ended questions that helps you both guide the conversation and explore how you can meet your client's needs. Both types are necessary and both are needed for successful conversations as long as each question is used intentionally for its specific objective.

Closed-ended questions play an important role because they're the best way to check for acceptance. Throughout a conversation, you need to check if you are on the same page as your client. For example, "Does that sound correct?" You also need to make sure they are engaged in the conversation and you haven't lost them. "Are you with me?" One of the key components of active listening is paraphrasing and then checking that your paraphrase was accurate and got the essence and meaning of their communication. Conversely, you can't know if a point you made or suggestion you put forth was truly accepted until you check.

Here are several examples of closed-ended questions that you could use to check for acceptance:

- Do you see what I mean?
- Does that resonate with you?
- Do you get where I'm going?
- Have I been clear?
- Have I made my point?
- Do you follow my train of thought?
- Do you agree?
- Do you disagree?
- Would you like me to continue?
- Do you accept what I've put forward?
- Do you feel the same way?
- Do you feel differently?

Becoming comfortable with different sequences of the two major question types comes from intentional practice.

Conceptually speaking, I like to draw an analogy with beach volleyball. In a game of two-person beach volleyball the two teammates work together to hit the ball over the net. A team is allowed three touches. The first touch is called a bump where the receiving player passes to his teammate. The second is called a set. The second player passes the ball back to a spot where the first player can spike it over the net.

I like to contrast the set of moves of bump-set-spike with the back and forth that occurs in the game of tennis. If you're playing conversational tennis with your client, the two of you are hitting the conversation content back and forth. The expressions, questions and answers may be related (or completely unrelated), but you're not collaborating. Bump-set-spike means you move to the same side of the net as your client and you work together to hit the ball over the net.

Here's an example of a brief tennis-like exchange I might have with my wife, Wendy, when I get home from work:

Ivan: "Did you have a good day?" [closed-ended question]

Wendy: "Not really."

Ivan: "Do you want to go out to dinner?" [closed-ended question]

Wendy: "I don't feel like it. Didn't I just tell you I didn't have a good day?" [closed-ended question]

Closed-ended questions alone reduce the likelihood for understanding and cause a conversation to be short. The ball quickly hits the net.

Let's try that again beach volleyball style with bump-set-spike:

Ivan: "How was your day?" [open-ended question]

Wendy: "Not too good."

Ivan: "What do you mean?" [open-ended, bump]

Wendy: "My co-workers were in a bad mood."

Ivan: "Do you want to talk about it?" [closed-ended, set]

Wendy: "Not really."

Ivan: "Okay." [bump]

Wendy: "Thanks for not making me talk about it. I just need a diversion."

Ivan: "What would a good diversion be?" [open-ended, set]

Wendy: "Takeout dinner and watch a movie at home."

Ivan: "Sounds perfect. Should I call the restaurant now?" [closed-ended, spike]

Wendy: "Yes, please." [Agreement]

A key part of the sequence happened when instead of using the closed-ended question, "Do you want to go out to dinner?" I used the open-ended question, "What do you mean by a diversion?" Instead of trying to propose a solution with a closed-ended question, I kept it open and let Wendy determine the solution. We didn't have to do the back-and-forth of guessing for solutions: "Do you want to go out to dinner?" No. "Do you want to see a movie?" No. "Do you want to do takeout and watch a movie at home?" Yes. All of the back-and-forth can be skipped over by asking one open-ended clarifying question. She selected the perfect solution for her which made it the perfect solution for me too. Your clients will also suggest solutions. The major benefit is clients are completely bought in to their own proposals.

Through teaching others how to ask open-ended questions and having thousands of conversations around the topic of money and finance, I've developed muscle memory on guiding conversations with certain sequences. If there is a path I want to go down or question I want answered, I know how to get to it no matter what the initial response is. Like a highly skilled pool player, each shot successfully sets up the next one.

It helps that I'm committed to a collaborative approach and even when I feel it's necessary to represent an opposing point of view in a conversation I do it in such a way that I put myself on the same side of the table (or net in my analogy) to evaluate the merits of his point of view. It's: "Let's look at the validity of your thought or position versus the validity of another thought or position."

Ask a closed-ended question and almost all of the time you're going to get one of four answers: yes, no, I don't know, or maybe.

So, when I ask a closed-ended question, most likely I'll be following it with an open-ended one—especially if they didn't give the answer I was looking for. I will want to find out the reason, motivation or why behind their initial answer.

Example of what happens when you start with a closed-ended question:

> Ivan: "Are you coming to the seminar?" [closed-ended]
>
> Client: "Yes."
>
> Ivan: "Great."

Another example:

> Ivan: "Are you coming to the seminar?" [closed-ended]
>
> Client: "I don't know yet."
>
> Ivan: "How come?" [open-ended]

You could get a multitude of answers. Some possibilities:

Client:

a) "I have to check my calendar at home."

b) "I'm too busy."

c) "I have too much going on."

It makes sense to follow up with an open-ended question (or questions) because you still need more information:

Ivan:

a) "What's your schedule been like lately?" [open-ended]

b) "What's making you so busy?" [open-ended]

c) "What kinds of things do you have going on?" [open-ended]

The point here is there are sequences that forward the action and sequences that complete the action. Usually a closed-ended question will be followed with an open-ended one to get more information and discover motivation (i.e. questions such as: How come? How so? Why's that? What makes you say that?). After paying attention to my question types for so many years, I've become really comfortable with these sequences.

What I've witnessed consistently is when a relationship manager leans too heavily on closed-ended questions, he tends to give up after asking only a few of them and is less effective. Here's a typical sequence:

Ivan: "Are you coming to the seminar?" [Closed-ended]

Client: "I don't know..."

Ivan: "Is it because you're too busy?" [Closed-ended]

Client: "Not really..."

Ivan: "Is it because you're not interested?" [Closed-ended]

Client: "No."

A point I'd like to make about asking three closed-ended questions in a row is you don't typically learn very much. If you follow a closed-ended question with two open-ended questions, you're able to gather additional information and can keep going. In the second example above, I asked three closed-ended in a row and now I likely have to move on. A series of three closed-ended questions in a row that each result in a "no" response closes off opportunities to ask more questions. I asked a closed-ended question and he answered in a closed-off fashion. He's not going to the seminar and he's not likely to tell me the reason. But a "yes" answer often closes things off as well. Relationship manager: "Do you know about the special offer we're having?" Client: "Yes."

Here's a different example:

Ivan: "How much do you know about the upcoming seminar?" [Open-ended]

Client: "I know it's scheduled for next month."

Ivan: "What do you think about going?" [Open-ended]

Client: "I haven't made up my mind yet."

Ivan: "How come?" [Open-ended]

Client: "I need to see my schedule first."

Ivan: "I understand. I would encourage you to attend. What would be the best way for me to follow up?" [Open-ended instead of something like, "Do you want me to follow up with you?]

Client: "You can contact me in a couple of weeks."

Ivan: "I'll do that. Do you want a phone call or email?" [Closed-ended to confirm his specific preference.]

In this dialogue, there were four open-ended questions in a row followed by a fifth closed-ended question. This kind of interchange could have gone many different directions. There's no magic sequence for all situations, but as discussed earlier, it's likely you're going to have to ask more open-ended questions than you've been asking. Once you become aware of this, I expect you'll start to catch yourself using closed-ended questions. I still catch myself. So, even if I'm in the middle of asking a question, when I realize I'm asking a closed-ended question when I should be asking an open-ended one, I will rephrase or restate it to make sure I'm using the right type for the answer I need.

To switch to a different kind of a conversation, such as when a client informs you he's leaving you for another company, I might instinctually find myself asking, "Are you making a change because of _____?" and then immediately stop myself and restart: "What's causing you to make this change?" or "What's prompting you to make this change right now?" I don't want to be guessing why he wants to make the change. There's a limited number of questions I'll be able to ask in this situation and I don't want to get into a multiple guess situation or irritate him because that will shut the window. I realize I need to hear it in his words because a guessing game is inefficient and counterproductive.

Example of a closed-ended multiple guess sequence:

1. Are you switching companies because of fees? No.
2. Are you switching because of our track record? No.
3. Are you switching because of bad service? No.
4. None of the above? Correct

One open-ended question, "What led you to make this decision?" or "How did you make this decision?" can leapfrog over four closed-ended questions which get you nowhere.

The best way to discover the client's rationale is to ask questions that encourage him to share it with you. When you lean on closed-ended questions, you wind up closing things off instead of opening things up. If you go to ask a question and find "do you?" or "are you?" starting to come out of your mouth remember this basic tip: start (or restart) your question with "what" or "how." It will give you a much better chance of asking a good open-ended question. But again, one type isn't better than the other. It's the intentional sequencing of both types that allows you to use questions skillfully. You don't want to close the window on the discussion at a pivotal time.

Conclusion

Questions are the pathway to helping your client understand his needs and discover ways to address them. Your client's answers to your questions (or even his own questions) are more influential than your answers. Telling him what to think is fundamentally different than him telling you what he thinks—the latter has so much more power.

As a relationship manager, you make your job more difficult when you don't use enough questions because while it's possible he may tell you everything you need to know without you asking questions, it's also highly unlikely. Asking questions in a specific way will help you attain your goals and meet your objectives. The bottom line is you will be better at your job if you learn to use questions skillfully.

Challenge yourself to use questions in a strategic fashion. Take advantage of what questions can do to increase the impact in your conversations. After all that I've learned, I wouldn't even think about entering a conversation without asking questions. It would be like leaving the house without my pants on. Also, when you become comfortable with how and when to use open-ended versus closed-ended questions, an added benefit will be your newfound ability to guide the direction of a conversation. The conventional thinking is the person talking in a conversation is in control of it, but I've come to believe that it's the person asking the questions who is truly in control.

Once you've asked a question in a skillful manner, now you need to make sure you listen. Speaking of listening...

Lesson 3 · Listen

GOOD LISTENING DIRECTLY IMPACTS client satisfaction. Your clients place tremendous value on being heard. If they don't feel listened to, they're going to be hard pressed to be satisfied or very satisfied with you and your company. Poor listening greatly increases the likelihood that they'll be dissatisfied overall. This makes listening fundamentally important because while good listening helps retain your clients and grows their relationships with you, poor listening results in dissatisfied clients, mediocre relationships and loss of business opportunities.

We've all had the experience of trying to communicate an idea or information to another person and midway through the conversation realize he hasn't heard a word we've said. Even if it's not his intention to ignore what we're saying, the distraction can make us feel slighted, frustrated or annoyed. We may even come away from the conversation thinking less of him. It's simply not conducive or constructive to open and trustworthy communication.

Raise your hand if you think you could become a better listener. Even though I can't see you right now, I think I just saw you raise your hand. I know I stopped typing just so I could raise mine. Because no matter how well I listen, I know I could always do better.

Have you ever gone to the doctor and before you even finish telling him why you're there, he interrupts you and tells you what he thinks the problem is and what to do about it? His assessment might be right, but you may be left feeling that his bedside manner could use some improvement.

You could be saying to yourself, "Wait doc, I haven't even finished telling you where it hurts!" As a relationship manager, your client's satisfaction doesn't always come from you giving him the right product or service or having all the right answers. Your bedside manner counts too. Poor listening is at the root of a poor bedside manner.

Your life is probably full of examples of people trying to help you without first listening to your problems, challenges and needs. Think about situations in your life when before you've been fully heard, the salesperson or relationship manager proceeds as if he already knows what you need. Now ask yourself, "How often do I do the same?" Unfortunately, it may be more often than you'd like to admit.

Hearing simply happens. Listening, however, is something you must consciously choose to do. The common belief is you're actively engaging in a conversation when you're talking and that when you're listening you're being passive. But good listening means being active too. If done well, you're actively receiving, processing, interpreting, comprehending and guiding with powerful intentions. As a relationship manager, listening is a skill you can and must develop. No matter how well you listen, it's safe to say, you could probably listen better and more comprehensively.

A Doctor's Pain

A client named Dr. Paine, who was generally satisfied with my company, approached my manager and voiced his concern that his relationship manager didn't understand him. He said, "He's very professional, articulate and conscientious, but it's gotten to a point where I don't want to work with him anymore." Dr. Paine was very committed to helping his patients deal with their physical pain. Paradoxically he suffered from a lot of pain himself with regard to his financial history. He'd been a victim of a fraudulent investment scheme and had panicked and sold his securities for pennies on the dollar during a bear market.

The problem was, over the past few years he tried to voice his concerns to his relationship manager Bart. Bart's response was to continue to try and reassure the doctor that his financial plan was sound and that he was in good hands. Bart was thoughtful and well spoken, but in his attempt to ease Dr. Paine's worry, he rarely stopped talking. Bart thought the way he'd reassure him was to repeat important concepts. He thought he was telling him what he needed to hear, but Dr. Paine stopped listening to him because he didn't feel heard himself. While it pained him to ask for a new relationship manager, he didn't want to switch companies, but felt he could no longer work with Bart.

My manager suggested he work with a new relationship manager and asked me to take over. In our introductory conversation, I asked one question: "What you would like me to know about you?" Then I simply encouraged him to talk. He talked for an hour and shared the important things he wanted me to know. My primary goal was for him to feel heard and understood. Naturally, listening intently was the best way to accomplish my goals. By making a conscious effort to listen, I helped him feel understood—it was the best prescription for his pain.

Stop Bad Listening Habits

We all know that to be healthy we need to eat right and exercise, but knowing what to do doesn't mean we'll do it. Listening is to relationship management what exercising and eating right is to optimal health. If you're going to become a better listener, you can start by eliminating bad behaviors.

Consider asking yourself this list of questions:

1. Do I give 100% of my attention to my client when he's speaking or am I frequently distracted?

2. When he's talking, do I often wish I was talking instead of him?

3. Do I give signs that I'm not listening by looking at my watch, my phone or shuffling through papers?

4. Do I sometimes pretend to listen but instead work on something else like reading my email?

5. Do I assume I already know what he's going to say and try to finish his sentences for him if he hesitates?

6. Do I ever find myself speaking over him?

7. Do I focus on where I disagree, or do I fully consider the merits of what he's saying?

8. Do I make it clear I value his experience, perspective and opinion?

9. Do I try to change the topic before he's finished with the current one?

Being a bad listener makes it challenging for your client to express himself. Serve your client well by not engaging in the behaviors that inhibit his communication with you.

Here are a few signs that you're not listening well to your client:

1. He's getting irritated and may even say, "You're not letting me finish."

2. You're rushing with your follow-up questions. He'll say, "I was coming to that."

3. He is rushing to answer your questions because he's afraid that you might interrupt him if he hesitates.

4. When you recap the conversation or paraphrase his words he continuously says, "No, I didn't say that." or "That's not what I meant."

I Don't Mean to Interrupt, But...

Growing up, I heard lots of stories of how, as a young man, my grandfather would spend his days roaming around the streets of Philadelphia looking for problems to solve.

My grandfather once approached an interaction that was on the verge of becoming a fight. He saw a boy stuttering, "You look aw-aw-aw-ful…." The boy got stuck on the word "awful" and it nearly got him beat up. My grandfather jumped in and said, "Let him finish." Although he was still stuttering, the boy was able to continue and said, "You look aw-aw-ful-ly familiar." It wasn't an insult at all, it was an attempt to establish rapport. Obviously, there is a significant difference between "You look awful" and

"You look awfully familiar" and that's why it's important to let people finish and it's essential to becoming a proficient listener.

Instead of waiting for people to finish, it's common to say something like, "I don't mean to interrupt, but…" Think about how inauthentic this is. If the intention wasn't to interrupt, why did he just do it?

Catching yourself interrupting is harder than catching other people doing it—especially when they're interrupting you. However, when you pay close attention, you'll notice interruptions happen all day long—both to you and by you.

There are several reasons why interruptions happen so frequently:

1. We're in a hurry. We think we can be more efficient with our time if our conversations move at a faster pace.

2. When someone is searching for a word, we try to help him by guessing it instead of waiting for him to find it.

3. We're busy thinking about what we're going to say next, or when we think we have something really good to say, we're afraid we might forget it.

4. We haven't truly committed to listening and have developed the bad habit of interrupting frequently.

5. We're competing for power, dominance and control. The meaning of one person interrupting another could be the equivalent of "What I have to say is more important than letting you finish." In essence, "I am more important than you."

There are three major negatives of interrupting your client:

1. It's rude. It violates the Golden Rule of, "Do unto others as you would have them do unto you." If you don't like being interrupted, it follows that your client doesn't like it either.

2. Interrupting your client breaks his flow and likely frustrates him. It increases the likelihood you'll miss out on the valuable information he was about to share with you.

3. It's more challenging to help your client get what he needs when you haven't let him fully communicate his needs.

You can become a better listener right away when you commit to stop interrupting or, at the very least, reduce the frequency. For most of us, it would be a major behavioral change to stop doing what we've been doing habitually and unconsciously for most of our lives. However, if you're committed to becoming a better listener, not interrupting is a great place to start.

Strategies to Stop Yourself from Interrupting/Talking

I've learned over and over again that if I'm going to listen intentionally, I need to have an active mechanism to keep myself from talking. Purposeful listening strategies will only make a difference in your relationships if you're able to implement them. You can't listen when you're talking, so here's a list of fourteen ways you can stop yourself from talking:

1. Bite your tongue, lip or inside of your cheek.
2. Put your fist to your mouth (like Rodin's famous statue, The Thinker) or one or two fingers on your lips.
3. Have a glass of water nearby and take a sip of water when you would normally be compelled to say something.
4. Sit on your hands. (This sounds odd at first, but it is a good reminder—especially for people who do a lot of talking with their hands.)
5. Turn your head to the side slightly such that one of your ears is closer to the person you're talking with.
6. Put a rubber band around your wrist and when you catch yourself interrupting or talking when you should be listening, give yourself a snap.
7. Hold a small object (a rock or a marble) in your hands to remind yourself to listen.
8. At the risk of developing a different bad habit, put a pen in your mouth.
9. If you're on the phone, put yourself on mute so you must press a button to say something.

10. To make sure the other person has finished completely, count to three slowly before you start talking.

11. Take notes. Focus on capturing key words and phrases.

12. If you can have a mentor or coach listen to your conversations, have them give you a signal to stop talking.

13. Look at a clock or a stopwatch. Challenge yourself to go longer and longer periods without talking.

14. At times you especially want to let your client talk, say to yourself, "I'm listening now."

Listen with an Intention in Mind

A relationship manager will typically approach a conversation with an agenda or a list of topics he wants to talk about. What about turning that around and having a specific focus for listening? You may find it helpful to pick one or more of the following intentions depending on the conversation and your commitment to this concept.

Listen to Receive

Approach the conversation such that you put yourself in a spot where you're open and ready to receive your client's communication. Your main goal is for your client to feel you have received his communication and only that. Receiving goes a long way and can be used in many specific situations. One time it's especially important is when your client is upset.

- Listen without responding. Resist the temptation to say something in return.
- Note or write down key words.
- Listen with your whole body.
- Wait awhile until you're sure he's done, let him fully unpack.

Listen to Understand Thinking

Be committed to learning his perspective and point of view. Focus on the assertions, declarations, facts and figures. No matter how different your point of view is, don't rebut or counter his statements. Simply seek to understand:

- What's his perspective, frame of reference or core position?
- What are the key supporting points for what he's attempting to communicate?
- Where's his point of view coming from?
- What's interesting about what he's saying?

Listen for Feelings

Set aside rationality or perspective and listen for the feelings your client is experiencing and trying to communicate to you. This intention is worthwhile when your client is upset or emotional. He may have a strong opinion for what needs to happen in a situation or may be driven by a strong emotion like anger or fear.

- Note how his emotions show through his body language, tone, pace and manner.
- Consider how you would feel if the same circumstances happened to you.
- Seek to empathize and let him fully verbalize his feelings.
- Give him space to be. Don't make the emotions (or being emotional) wrong.

Listen to Collaborate

As a relationship manager, one of your missions is to help your client articulate his goals, objectives, thoughts and feelings. There will be times when you might find yourself with conflicting goals because you either must comply with your company's rules or pursue business objectives that might not be in his best interest. Avoid turning the conversation into a competition, instead:

- Consider yourself as being on the same team as your client.
- Listen for the objectives you have in common.
- Listen for information that will help you solve his problems, provide excellent service and present optimal solutions.

Listen with Respect

Show respect by giving your client the opportunity to speak without being interrupted and treat his words with importance. Encourage him to express himself and watch with admiration. Focus on his good traits and find things to honor. Allow yourself to leave your own world and jump into his world to learn how interesting and amazing it is to be him. Witness his greatness. One of the most important gifts you can give to another is your listening and respect.

- Consider what his contributions to the world are.
- Wonder about his achievements and the adversity he's overcome.
- Think about all the people he means something to.
- Give him the same importance you would give to a family member or a close friend.
- If you were going to write the forward to his life story, what positive things would you say?

Talking Over A Tycoon

Early in my career, I went on an appointment with a veteran salesman named Matt. We were meeting with a real estate tycoon named John. We understood that John was looking for a new bank to handle his financing needs and we wanted to make sure our company was chosen.

From my perspective, the purpose of this first appointment was to listen to John—especially because he'd indicated he was only beginning to consider a change in banks. And, even though Matt and I agreed before the meeting that we'd mostly ask questions and listen, Matt went on autopilot throwing out the same salesy phrases he'd been using for years.

At one point in the conversation, when Matt paused for a second, I interjected a simple question: "What can we do to help you?" Before John could finish his thought, Matt started talking over him. The perfect opportunity to help John discover his needs was undercut by Matt's inclination to talk too much.

When I had a second opportunity, I asked John, "Is there anything you need that you're not currently getting?" John said he didn't think so, but wasn't finished answering when he was interrupted again by Matt with empty and meaningless boasts about our bank. I kept thinking this was a time to find out more about John's needs and what he saw as the benefits of potentially working with us.

The problem was Matt wouldn't stop talking and as a result we made very little progress in learning about John's needs. Luckily, a few weeks later, I was able to schedule a second meeting with John. Because Matt wasn't a part of the second meeting, I was able to fully listen. For two hours, I simply asked questions and let John answer them. I took three pages of notes. I dug deep and as a result, better understood John's personal and professional history which also helped him to feel that I cared about him instead of just caring about getting his business.

This taught me how important it is to take a stand and make space to listen. It's commonly believed that selling is the same as talking, but it's not. Highly-effective relationship managers know that listening is the most important part of their job. Alfred Brendel said, *"The word **listen** has the same letters as the word **silent**."* If you're silent right now, you can hear how profound that idea is.

To check that your client feels you are listening well, you could ask him for feedback with questions such as:

1.   How well do you feel I listen to you?

2.   How important is it for me to listen to you?

3.   What helps you to know I'm listening?

Talk yourself out of talking too much. First century Greek philosopher Epictetus said, *"We have two ears and one mouth so that we can listen twice as much as we speak."*

Implement Basic Active Listening Strategies

Listening is not a passive activity. If you've ever gone to see a psychologist, therapist or counselor, you may have noticed that instead of talking most of the time, he listens actively. This is key because when he listens well it makes it easier for you to talk.

When you listen actively, you enable your client to tell you more about his needs. When you understand his needs, you can help to satisfy them. When you're not listening, you can only guess what your client needs. You may be right some of the time, but you'll increase your understanding by becoming a better listener.

Whenever I can remember to be an active listener in my conversations, they seem to go better, are easier to manage, take less effort and help my clients feel understood, liked and valued.

Here are four easy and simple techniques to implement active listening:

1. Short responses

When your client has a lot to say or you want him to say more, use a short response:

- Really?
- Oh?
- Interesting
- I see/hear you.
- Go on

One, two or three-word statements invite them to keep going. Hearing something encouraging is reassuring. Short responses are helpful when someone is emotional or upset. Sometimes you just don't know what to say but a couple of words—and not more—can make all the difference. Too many words can stifle your client's self-expression and inhibit the communication he needs to deliver to you.

2. Echoing

Echoing is repeating back to your client what he just said with some (or all) of the exact same words he just said. It's a basic way to confirm you've heard what he said without stopping the flow of his communication to you. He may say something like: "I'm upset with your company's service." I might respond, "You're upset with our company's service." If said sincerely and from a caring place, he'll feel heard and it encourages him to continue.

3. Short questions

Short questions (generally seven words or less) prevent you from turning questions into statements and make it much clearer that you're asking a question and will listen to the response. It's easy to assume you've understood what your client meant, but a short follow-up question offers him a chance to clarify and elaborate. It's a false assumption he truly knew what he meant. We think people are telling us what they mean the first time around, but I'm amazed at how people restate or even contradict themselves when I ask, "What do you mean by that?" or "When you said ____, what did you mean?" Take the point of view that the first version of a story or explanation is just a draft. When you follow up, you'll be amazed at how it will change and so will he. "Please elaborate" or "Tell me more" are other ways to get another version of the story.

4. Restating

Paraphrase what you just heard in your own words. When you add your own words and interpretation, you can both validate his concerns while also setting the stage for solutions you'll propose later in the conversation. "You're upset with our service and want to know what we're going to do about it. Am I correct?" or "Tell me if I'm wrong, but you're upset with our service and your expectations were unmet?"

Listening requires patience and hard work but it's a worthy endeavor. In a world where talk is abundant, true listening is rare. Practice basic active listening strategies. It's a quick and effective way to improve your listening skills immediately.

Create a Balance Between Listening and Talking

One way to think about listening versus talking is within a framework where you evaluate one person's dominance over another. Consider three zones on a continuum:

Zone 1 You dominate the conversation	Zone 2 You both talk and listen	Zone 3 Your client dominates the conversation
You do a majority of the talking as if you were a teacher.	There is a good balance between speaking and listening.	The client does almost all the talking. You become like a student.
You dominate the conversation and hardly let your client get a word in edgewise. Because he feels dominated, he isn't satisfied with the conversation. He's likely frustrated.	You're talking and listening about half of the time. The conversation feels comfortable since you're both having the opportunity to talk and be heard.	You can't find an opening to talk. Because you're the one being dominated, you become frustrated. You feel like you have no control of where the conversation is going.
Rapport is weak. It's hard to match his verbal communication because there's not very much of it.	Neither of you are dominating the conversation. You're able to have a collaborative and productive exchange of information and ideas.	You might get a lot of information as he's talking but it might not be the information you need.
The more you talk, and the more knowledge and information you provide, the less he can absorb.	You're able to get and give feedback. There is an openness to the conversation.	You can't demonstrate your value, be consultative or address his objections.
At some point in being dominated, without being given the chance to respond, he stops listening to you and is more inclined to dislike you.	He finds you likeable and trustworthy. You have an enjoyable conversation.	You have trouble liking him because he's not letting you talk or do your job.

Unfortunately, many relationship managers are responsible for spending too much time in the first zone. Fortunately, most conversations have a semblance of balance. While it's rare that your client completely dominates the conversation, when he does, it's unpleasant. It gives you a taste for how a client may feel when you dominate a conversation with him.

Do what you can to steer the conversation into zone two and out of zones one and three. The good news is most conversations have balance to a degree. The better you are at creating balance between listening and talking, the more control you'll have over your conversations. A focus on listening with intention gets you out of zone one. Depending on your client's personality, getting out of zone three can be more challenging, but it can be done with certain types of questions which we'll discuss later in the book.

Conclusion

Improve your listening skills and you'll find your conversations will be easier for you. You won't have to shoulder the responsibility for doing all the talking. Also, listening is a proven strategy to help you establish (or reestablish) rapport. Clients like conversing with you when you let them talk and they're able to fully express themselves.

Improve your listening skills and you'll see a direct impact on your business results. Moreover, if you're listening poorly it means you're likely missing out on a whole host of good stuff.

Listening has been proven to deepen your relationships, increase their quality, and enhance their fullness. The better you listen, the better you will be in creating powerful connections with your clients. Good listening skills are one of the best ways to retain your clients and poor listening skills are one of the best ways to lose them. A huge part of making people feel good about talking with you results from how you listen to them. The bottom line is if you improve your listening skills, you'll be more effective in serving your clients and meeting your company's objectives.

Now that you have a few tools for improving your listening skills, something you can specifically do with your listening ability is to focus on your client's needs.

Lesson 4 • Focus on Needs

AS A RELATIONSHIP MANAGER, you can't always give your client what he wants, but if he finds he doesn't get what he needs from you, he will probably seek it from someone else.

Forget what your company offers for a moment and simply think about what you offer in a relationship with your client. Consider yourself the product. Because as a relationship manager, you don't control what the competition does or the decisions your company makes about its products or services. What you do have control over is how you conduct yourself in the conversations you have with your clients. You can be a resource that transcends the resources your company has available. Consider yourself as an additional value-added product or service that is separate and distinct from your company's offer—a combination where 1+1 is much greater than 2.

My belief is you satisfy needs by who you're being. Here are 18 ways to accomplish that:

1. Be trustworthy. Be someone who conducts himself with integrity and speaks with honesty and directness.

2. Be reliable. Be someone who does what he says he will do and be accessible when needed.

3. Be responsive. Make it a practice to return a voicemail message the same day—if not within a couple of hours or less. If you can't get back to him the same day, send an email or a text at the end of the day saying when you will.

4. Be interesting and personable. Your client wants to like you and have interesting conversations with you.

5. Be someone who discusses philosophy and wisdom. Develop a relationship that goes beyond the product or service you represent and helps him to consider larger truths.

6. Be a good translator and communicator. Most clients have the need for someone to explain complex products and concepts in a simple way.

7. Be a friend. Some of your clients don't have a lot of friends. Even though you're in a business relationship, you may be able to meet some of their need for friendship. It's much harder to end a business relationship with someone you consider to be a friend.

8. Be someone who provides choices. Without choices your client may see you as inflexible. He might feel constrained by not having more than one path to follow.

9. Be understanding, caring and empathetic. You may care deeply about your client, but without the skill to put yourself in his shoes, he may not experience it. Your client needs to feel understood.

10. Be someone who shows respect, listens and provides validation. Even if you have to take an opposing position, you need to be able to do it while validating your client at the same time to help him avoid feeling embarrassed.

11. Be someone who makes your company's offer easy or easier to use. The products and services companies create are not always the easiest to use.

12. Be someone who instills confidence and peace of mind. Anxiety is not something your client needs more of. If he has reason to believe you're not going to be able to deliver some of what you've promised, he may be anxious or doubtful that you can deliver any of it.

13. Be someone who provides valuable advice and guidance. A client who comes to you seeking advice will be disappointed if you don't provide any.

14. Be detail-oriented. Missing details quickly undermines your credibility.

15. Be inclusive. Including a client in your thinking and in decision-making helps him feel he belongs and is acknowledged.

16. Be an aggressive problem solver. It's an absolute certainty that problems will happen. A client greatly appreciates when he has someone who will aggressively and quickly act to solve them.

17. Be loyal and committed. When you are loyal and committed to your client, he is more likely to be loyal and committed to you.

18. Be someone who helps your client look good and avoid looking bad.

The items on the above list may seem obvious, but it's rare to find someone who exemplifies and embodies all of them. Use this list as a reminder of who you can be such that you satisfy your client's need for an excellent relationship manager. Doing so will create tremendous loyalty. Moreover, the measure of whether or not you're being a certain way is not if you attempted to be that way, but that your client experiences you that way. The ultimate test is receiving acknowledgement from the client such as, "I feel I can trust you. You're reliable, dependable and solve the problems I bring you. You help me get what I need."

I remember one time I was talking with my colleague Kevin at the water cooler. He told me he'd been focusing on establishing rapport and listening better, but when I suggested he focus on his client's needs in every conversation he asked me, "What if they don't have any needs?" My reaction was incredulous: "How is that possible?" It was a watershed moment for me because I realized the way I think about clients' needs was fundamentally different than most of my colleagues.

As a standard way of speaking with clients, most relationship managers will ask a client if he has any questions. Typically, the response is no. This was the case for Kevin. He said he'd ask and the client would say something like, "No, I don't have any questions right now. I don't need anything. I'm good." and Kevin would say, "Okay, let me know if you do." This is a very standard interchange between a relationship manager and a client.

The problem I saw was he was missing out on opportunities to address and satisfy needs because he wasn't aware of what he was looking for. Client relationships are put at risk this way because a relationship manager takes for granted that if a client has something he needs, he'll voice it. Accepting "I don't need anything." at face value is a mistake. I've learned the client who says, "I don't need anything." isn't trying to be misleading, he's just not being realistic—everyone has needs!

The key lesson is to focus on your client's needs and put them first. When you focus on your or your company's needs first, you:

1. create distance between you and your client,
2. reduce your interpersonal connection,
3. diminish the overall impact of your conversations, and
4. undermine the level of trust.

Building rapport, using questions skillfully and listening well make it much more likely your client will share what his needs are with you. When you focus on your client's needs and give them your full attention, your conversations will become much more productive and will result in greater client satisfaction.

This is important because from your company's point of view, your purpose as a relationship manager is to retain clients and sell them more products or services. A client is much more likely to buy when he's been made aware of something he needs. From the client's point of view, a relationship manager's job is to simplify his relationship with your company and meet his needs. Focusing on needs accomplishes both.

Discuss the Needs Hidden Behind the Topic

Typical conversations default to topics and subjects. For example, you might discuss what's in the news. You might discuss account information, your company's offerings or how you're different from your competition. But if that's all you do, when will you discuss their needs?

Some of your discussions will touch lightly on a topic and some will go into a fair bit of depth. Some of those conversations may be interesting and some may be downright boring. Sometimes you'll agree and other times you will take an oppositional point of view. But behind or underneath all the words is a basic truth that we all have needs that have to be met. Understanding what your client's needs are is your North Star. You can and must orient yourself and the conversation around your client's needs.

When you focus on a topic and try to do a good job of addressing the topic, you might completely miss satisfying your client's actual needs. Just because a client asked you to comment about something in the news or what's happening at your company doesn't mean he truly wants or needs you to talk about it. It's counterintuitive that a client would ask about something that he doesn't really want to talk about, but I've found that to be the norm instead of the exception.

Talking about the topic he mentioned is like considering the tip of the iceberg to be the entire iceberg. Effective conversations may start with the visible part of the iceberg (the topic) but you need to proceed to the part of the iceberg under the water where your client's needs are located. You may not be aware of them, but—as I told Kevin—they're there. I'm not saying you don't have to be somewhat knowledgeable about the topic they bring up, but you need to focus on the needs underneath the topic to be most effective. Otherwise you will get lost in the topic and never address what's most important to him.

I Asked You About the Stock Market but I Really Care About Something Else

Out of the blue, Linda called me for the first time ever. I'd dealt with her husband, Michael, for ten years but had never spoken with her so I was surprised to receive her call. She said, "I need to talk with you about the stock market. I don't think all our money should be in stocks." I said, "Why do you say that?" She said, "My brothers think it's too risky for me. They're getting out of the market, but I don't know what to do."

I started to explain why we've recommended stocks to her husband for years and explained the rationale. I eloquently elaborated our firm's expertise. I went on for about 20 minutes before realizing she was growing more and more concerned. Against my better judgement, I indulged by talking about the topic she brought up when what I really needed to do was find out what she needed. There's a wide gap between a need for information and a need for emotional support.

I asked what caused her to call for the first time ever. She shared with me that her husband was showing the first signs of dementia and she realized she couldn't let him handle the finances on his own anymore. She was sad and scared, and by necessity, reluctantly becoming involved in the finances. As we delved into her circumstances, she shared what she needed was for me to understand the situation. She didn't need a lecture about economic forecasts, political analysis or price earnings ratios.

The lesson here is to consider the needs behind the topic. Focus on your client's needs instead of the topic he mentions first. By focusing on needs instead of on the topics mentioned, you'll alter the experience for your client. He'll feel you're truly helping him. Because your client doesn't care how much you know, he needs to know how much you care. You do that by focusing on his needs.

Make a note of the topic he brings up as a starting point, but find a way to ask what prompted him to raise the topic. This will lead the conversation down a productive path. If you indulge in the topic without understanding the reasons it was brought up, you'll be caught in a web. It's not that you completely avoid the topic—it's that if you stick solely to the topic you'll miss out on the real reason the topic was brought up.

In each conversation, ask yourself both: "Do I understand what my client's needs are?" and "Does he feel like I understand what his needs are?" While you may touch on the topic he brings up, don't fall into the whirlpool of a topic or content-based conversation. "What if he doesn't have any needs?" becomes, "I know my clients have needs and even if they can't think of any needs they have, I am prepared to help surface them." We all have needs.

Consider What All Human Beings Need

My thinking about what everyone needs has evolved over time and I've integrated different distinctions, concepts and frameworks. To provide some context, I'd like to share four major influences on my thinking:

1. Abraham Maslow

Abraham Maslow's Hierarchy of Needs. The hierarchy is typically depicted as a pyramid.

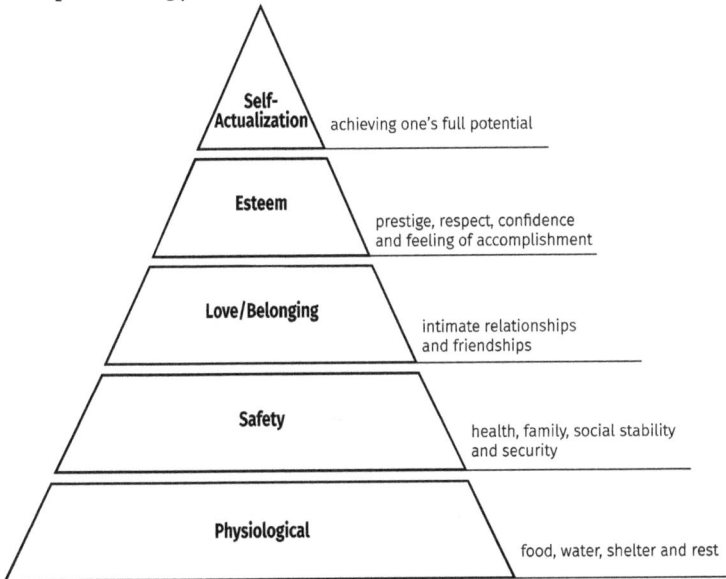

- **Self-Actualization** — achieving one's full potential
- **Esteem** — prestige, respect, confidence and feeling of accomplishment
- **Love/Belonging** — intimate relationships and friendships
- **Safety** — health, family, social stability and security
- **Physiological** — food, water, shelter and rest

Maslow's theory suggested that there are innate human needs that have to be fulfilled in a certain order. If a lower level need goes unmet, like being hungry, you can't focus on higher level needs like the need for esteem and respect from others.

2. David McClelland

David McClelland put forth a theory on human motivation which stated that people are driven by one of following three main motivators:

1. Need for achievement
2. Need for affiliation
3. Need for power

He didn't think a person is solely motivated by one of the needs but that everyone has a tendency toward one of the three needs.

3. Anthony Robbins

Anthony Robbins asserts there are six core human needs:

1. Certainty
2. Uncertainty/Variety
3. Significance
4. Love/Connection
5. Growth
6. Contribution

4. Landmark Education

Landmark Education distinguishes five key needs in a distinction called "already and always listening":

- The need to look good and avoid looking bad
- The need to be right and avoid being wrong
- The need to dominate and avoid domination
- The need to justify and avoid being unjustified
- The need to be valid and avoid being invalid

Considering your clients' needs on a human level is very important. If you understand what people need and what motivates them at a fundamental level, you have an advantage over your colleagues who don't—and most don't. Most relationship managers are focused on meeting their own needs or their company's current objectives. Over time, as you deepen your relationships, you'll find you can support your clients and help them meet more and more of their needs.

Conclusion

My goal in this chapter was to answer the question Kevin had for me, "What if the client doesn't have any needs?" and then demonstrate the great number of needs that can be addressed.

A common analogy is that peeling an onion is like peeling back the complexity of a problem or situation one layer at a time, but focusing on your client's needs may be more like peeling a pomegranate. If you've ever peeled one, it's a lot less straightforward than peeling an onion and better signifies the complexity of your client's needs. While an onion typically has 10-11 layers, a pomegranate has many sections and hundreds of seeds. In the same way, your clients have hundreds of little needs that you can discover and seek to meet over the course of a long-term relationship.

Consider that as a relationship manager—no matter what product or service your company sells—you add value to the degree that you focus on and satisfy the many needs your clients have. You're in the needs satisfaction business and must prioritize your client's needs accordingly. A client's surface level needs are only a place to start.

Switch your paradigm from getting your needs met to getting your clients' needs met. By making sure their needs are met you will get your needs met as well. Clients whose needs are met are more willing to reciprocate. Needs-based conversations allow you to collaborate with your clients in an effective and empowering fashion. They help your clients see you as an ally and as someone who cares about them on a deeper level—beyond the normal expectations they have for their business relationships.

Building rapport, asking questions skillfully, listening and focusing on needs provide access to a conversation that operates on a deeper level. But, these skills are of little value if you don't have the discipline and self-control to use them. Speaking of self-control...

Lesson 5 · Exercise Self-Control

HAVE YOU EVER looked back at a conversation and thought, "That could have gone better!" and wanted to start over again? I have—and I do—often.

Ideally, conversations with your clients would always go exactly the way you'd like, and you'd be able to directly influence your client's behavior. If that were the case, you'd always accomplish your goals. But, the reality is you can't control another person, you can only control yourself. What I am suggesting in this chapter is that in order to maximize control over a conversation you must be disciplined and exercise self-control. This means being responsible and accountable for the outcome and process but giving up an attachment to a certain result. This only happens with awareness of what's occurring in every conversation while it's happening. You're aware of what's occurring with him, with you, and in the conversation as a whole.

Great athletes have tremendous body control. It amazes me when a wide receiver leaps up in the air with a defender in his face, stretches his arms out and catches a pass, and while falling out of bounds, taps his toes in-bounds with the defender on top of him. In sports, physical body control scores points. In business, it's self-control.

You'll become an all-pro in your conversations to the degree that you can control what comes out of your mouth and how you listen. But it's more than listening just to hear the words—it's also listening for the other person's true self-expression. Providing a space for your client to express himself is a gift you can give him and it requires you to exercise self-control.

Moreover, a good portion of control comes from the actions we've already discussed in the book:

- Building rapport,
- Using questions skillfully, and
- Listening.

If you're intentional about how you conduct yourself and are disciplined during your conversations, it will make a significant difference. Because your main goal as a relationship manager is to retain and grow your client relationships, being able to influence and persuade your clients to take certain actions and behave in certain ways is paramount. Optimally, you're doing such a good job that your clients have simply stopped looking for an alternative—you're it and they're not leaving you. They'll go out of their way to bring you more business and be ambassadors for you.

Watch Your Behavior

There are hundreds of conversations I wish I could do over. Here's some of the things they had in common:

- I got defensive and angry. I lost my cool. I argued.
- I interrupted frequently and was frequently interrupted in return.
- I volunteered unnecessary information which led the conversation down the wrong path.
- I jumped around to different topics without completing any of them.
- I talked when I should have remained quiet and listened.
- The conversation went poorly because I didn't have a plan or clear objectives.

Even though it takes two to tango, as the relationship manager, you're 100% responsible for the dance. While you don't control the client's part of the conversation, it doesn't mean that you abdicate your responsibility for the outcome of the conversation.

How you control conversations is by controlling yourself and your behavior. If the conversation slips into an argument, it's on you. If it goes off track, it's on you. If you can't find anything to agree upon, it's on you. If after the conversation, you feel stupid, guilty, ashamed, defeated, angry or sad, it's on you. That's the bad news, but luckily, it's also the good news. It's the good news because you can learn how to exercise self-control in a conversation.

What does exercising self-control in a conversation look/sound/feel like?

- You're poised.
- You're following a plan.
- You're focused on the conversation.
- You're respectful.

In addition, awareness is key. Evaluate:

1. Your experience in the conversation,
2. Your client's experience, and
3. The conversation as a whole, as if you were an independent third party.

The major way to foster awareness during a conversation is to continually ask yourself questions from three different perspectives:

1. From your perspective:

- Have I established rapport and am I maintaining it?
- Am I listening well and asking sufficient questions?
- Am I in control or out of control?
- Am I operating from a place of intention?
- Am I talking at or with my client?

2. From the client's perspective:

- Is he enjoying the conversation or is he becoming irritated or annoyed with it?

- Does he seem comfortable or uncomfortable?

- Is he in an emotional state or a logical state?

- Is he engaged and engaging or disengaged and disengaging?

3. From the perspective of a 3rd party observer:

- How is this conversation going?

- Is the conversation on track or off track?

- Is the conversation being productive and moving forward or is it being counterproductive?

- Is the conversation moving toward agreement and alignment or growing disagreement and discord?

- Is the conversation fulfilling its goals and objectives or is it going in a completely different direction?

- Does the conversation have a purpose?

It takes time, practice and many repetitions to be able to consider all three perspectives at once, but our brains can do it—especially when you're prepared and have a plan to follow. That's exactly what we'll be discussing for the remainder of the book, but for now, there's more to say about exercising self-control.

Here are five behaviors to avoid:

1. Going Too fast: Gauge your speed to your client's tastes and preferences. Maybe your client operates at a slower pace than you do or needs you to slow down because the information you're providing is new or unfamiliar to him. If you sense you are out of sync, you can ask, "Am I going at the right pace for you?" Or go open-ended with, "How is this pace for you?"

2. Mismatching Volume: Watch being too loud or too quiet. Your voice can be overpowering such that your client is literally leaning backward away from you (or on the phone, holding it further away from his ears). When this happens, it creates an unnecessary distance between you and him. Sometimes when you think you're not getting through to your client, instead of thinking how you could be clearer in your explanation, you'll just speak louder and louder as if being louder would help him understand you better. If you're talking too quietly, (or the phone connection is bad) he won't be able to fully understand you.

3. Using insider language: It's easy to slip into using your industry's or company's jargon. Using acronyms can cause your clients to feel lost. Therefore, company acronyms shouldn't ever make it into your conversations with clients. It indicates you're not paying attention to the words you're selecting with regard to making yourself easy to understand. Much like being too fast or too loud, insider language creates distance between you and your client.

4. Repeating yourself: Repeating yourself because you don't think your client is understanding you is generally counterproductive and can frustrate him. I've observed many relationship managers repeating themselves because they haven't provided a clear and concise explanation. Many times however, it's not that you're being unclear, it's that the client doesn't accept what you've said and in attempting to convince him, you repeat yourself. Repeating what you've said over and over again as if to bludgeon him into acceptance is not going to work. Instead, you need to stop and ask an open-ended question such as, "What do you think?" or "What's your opinion?" Asking "What's your point of view?" can also prevent you from repeating yourself and creates a better understanding of why he doesn't accept the point of view you've put forth. Being willing to let his point of view just be, without trying to correct, it can also open up the space for a productive dialogue.

5. Wrong spotting: A common pitfall is reactively telling your client he's wrong. Since you're listening for whether you agree or disagree, or whether your client is right or wrong, it's common to let your inner voice blurt out, "That's wrong." and cut him off. Pointing out differences in the way you view something versus what is right or wrong can be much more productive. Consider the difference between saying, "What's wrong with our competition is _____." versus "What's different about us from our competition is _____." You can distinguish between two services of your respective companies (or different points of view) without being disparaging.

Get Feedback

At one point in my career, I worked at a company where part of the training program was to have a formal mentor. My mentor, Mark, was very hands-on. His job was to listen to all my phone conversations until he felt I was ready to have conversations independently. It was like I was learning to skydive with a tandem instructor.

This was an unwelcome experience. I had never had anyone scrutinize me so closely. I felt like I was under a microscope. I also learned I was more sensitive than I thought to what felt like constant criticism. At the time, I believed I was already very polished and professional, so I was taken aback by his blunt feedback. When I told my father about my experience, he said, "He doesn't sound like a mentor. He sounds like a tormentor."

Looking back however, I know Mark's feedback was spot-on and useful, but at the time, I thought the criticism was unfair and overly critical. The most challenging part was getting feedback on-the-fly in the middle of an actual conversation with a client.

At first I wore a phone headset with one earpiece so I could listen to my mentor's advice in real time during the conversation. While I was hearing my client in my right ear I would hear Mark talking in my left ear. What I quickly learned was it was way too distracting. It left me fumbling for words. I was unable to follow Mark and the conversation with my client at the same time. Things had to change. I couldn't continue this way.

I switched to a headset with two earpieces to make it harder for Mark to talk to me while I was talking with clients. Then I asked him to write his feedback out, noting he could still provide real-time feedback and suggestions but it would be less distracting. However, we quickly learned he couldn't write fast enough. The solution we negotiated was the development of hand signals. Most of his feedback was similar in nature and could be grouped into a limited number of concepts that he could easily communicate with a gesture. The signals communicated quickly, were easy to recognize, and didn't interfere with my train of thought.

The hand signals we used the most were:

Slow down	Signaled by two hands face down moving slowly downward two times
Speed up	Signaled by a hand moving in a circle as if it were reeling in a fish with a fishing rod
Keep it short	Signaled by two hands facing each other starting about 6 inches apart moving to about 3 inches
Stop talking	Signaled with a gesture to button his lips
Ask open-ended questions	Signaled with palms together opening like a book
Listen carefully	Signaled by pointing to an ear
Keep going/ you're doing well	Signaled by a thumbs up
Wrap up	Signaled by his hands making a motion as if he were tying up a bow

These eight signals made a big difference in helping me receive Mark's coaching. In addition, I found these key concepts generally kept me out of trouble and helped me gain more control over my conversations.

It's like when you're first learning to drive and the major ways to put yourself (and your driving instructor) at risk are going too fast or driving where you're not supposed to. These hand signals were exactly what I needed to stop me from talking too fast, talking too long and opening up subjects I wasn't actually prepared to discuss.

When you're nervous, there's a tendency to talk a lot and talk too fast. When you're talking without thinking about what you're saying, it's like your car is driving without you pushing the gas pedal. In this mode, you say things you haven't fully thought through. As a result, fillers (ums, ahs, y'knows) or unnecessary (or repetitive) words come out of your mouth because you are trying to maintain a pace to make yourself look good, but without stopping to reflect on what you're saying. When you hurry without knowing where you're going it undermines the strength of your communication and takes your conversation off track. You'll tend to take unconscious tangents which get both you and your client lost.

Keeping things short helps you avoid saying too much. More words and more repetition aren't necessarily better. They're just more. When you think you aren't communicating the right message, you can stop by pressing your brakes and ask something like, "Does that make sense?" It's like stopping and asking for directions when you're lost. There are many subjects you're not prepared to discuss. If you go too fast and off topic, you might find yourself in the wrong part of town.

When Mark gestured to me to button my lips, it was because he saw I could do more harm continuing to talk rather than stopping cold. While I might have been trying to solve a problem, he could see I was about to open up a can of worms. Since I hadn't had time to think things through, I was going to complicate things unnecessarily and create problems. You'll frequently see how people try to solve problems or research hard to find information in the middle of a conversation rather than simply suggesting, "Why don't I take the time to research this and get back to you?"

Most driving accidents happen because people aren't paying attention or anticipating what other drivers might do. Distracted driving is dangerous. So are distracted conversations. Moreover, when you don't listen enough or give the other person a chance to talk, you might as well be talking through the windows of different cars because you're not likely having the same conversation. If you pull up next to their car and ask them if they have any Grey Poupon mustard, but neither cars' windows are rolled down, you cannot hear them say anything, let alone, "But of course."

Demanding Retired Executive

Years ago, I took over a relationship with a retired executive, Jim. He had a reputation as being aggressive and demanding. When I began working with him, I quickly found this reputation was accurate. Greeting him was like getting hugged by a bear. He had me on my heels from the start of every conversation. He fired questions at me and I struggled to answer them.

Dealing with Jim was stressful. Because I knew he'd ask aggressive questions, I was reluctant to converse with him. Every time I talked with him, I simply wanted to make it through the conversation. I wanted the conversations to end. I wanted him to stop bombarding me with his relentless inquiries. When I had to speak with him, I thought, "What am I going to have to defend now?"

Everything changed when I was able to exercise self-control and not reflexively answer his questions. It helped me to integrate the other lessons I'd learned. How could I best build rapport? How could I become the one asking the questions? If I could listen and then turn the focus to his needs, I thought things would get better in our conversations and in our relationship. I was right.

I selected questions that he couldn't resist answering: "What was your life like growing up? What most shaped your beliefs? What were your parents like? Where do babies come from?" (The fourth question in this sequence was just to see if you're paying attention. I did not in fact ask him where babies come from.) As I asked each question he gladly answered and his answers became longer and longer. He warmed up to me and seemed to like me more. He stopped asking his questions with the same ferocity and accusatory tone and I no longer needed to be defensive because he stopped being on the attack.

Direct the Action

Wouldn't it be great if you could completely control your conversations? Of course it would! Here's the good news: metaphorically speaking, you can control them with a conversational remote-control. Keep these buttons in mind:

Rewind:

Rewind the conversation when it gets ahead of where it should be. When I sense this has happened, I might say, "Let's rewind the conversation a bit," or "Let's take a step back."

Examples of when you need to rewind:

- When you've skipped establishing rapport or rapport has gone out of the conversation
- When you've moved on to the next topic without completing the previous one
- When it appears you're having a different conversation than the one your client is having
- When you've gotten stuck in the details and need to look at the bigger picture
- When you've discussed next steps prematurely

Fast Forward:

Fast forward a conversation when it keeps slipping backward. An example of this is when you've covered the same topics multiple times. You're not being efficient or serving your client well by allowing the conversation to repeat itself. In a case like this I'll say things like, "I think we may have discussed this already. Is it okay if we move on?"

Examples of when to fast forward:

- When you've talked too long about non-business topics
- When it's taken too long to agree why you're having the conversation
- When you're repeating topics for no apparent reason
- When you've gotten stuck in too many details and need to move forward to resolving the situation

Play:

Play is the standard operating procedure in a conversation. Play means following your game plan. Rapport exists, you're using questions skillfully, you're listening well, you're focused on needs. You're being self-aware, strategic and exercising self-control.

Pause:

Pause a conversation when it's spiraling out of control or when your client is getting emotional in such a way that you're no longer working together. I'll say things like, "Let's pause for just a moment." or "Let's take a brief timeout." or "Why don't we take a brief recess?" (This lets both of us get our bearings and compose ourselves.)

Examples of when you need a pause in the conversation:

- When your client is constantly interrupting you (or vice versa) with an impatient or angry tone
- When things have become tense and you or your client have become emotional or defensive
- When you or your client are rushing or hurried
- When your client can't stick to (or focus on) the agreed upon agenda
- When the conversation is stuck, and you cannot come to any agreement

Stop:

An important part of controlling the action is by knowing when to simply stop talking. Have you ever noticed how other relationship managers tend to go on talking without stopping, barely breathing or asking a question? It shows a lack of self-awareness. Keeping track of how long you've talked by using a clock or stopwatch during a conversation can help you be disciplined.

When I'm doing a mock scenario with someone who tends to be long-winded, I'll time him. If he goes on talking for several minutes without inviting me to have a turn, even though I am trying to pay attention, I start tuning out. His words are washing over me and it's easy to become distracted, bored, disengaged or detached. In contrast, when he invites me to talk, I'm all of a sudden engaged. At the end of his long-winded soliloquy, I ask how long he thinks he's talked. Usually he has no idea, but appreciates me bringing awareness to his lack of awareness.

Using the remote-control buttons to maintain control of yourself and the conversation as a whole is a key to being successful. You can't control what your client will say, but by using your metaphorical remote-control you can act as the director and leader of the conversation. You and your client both benefit from your ability to manage and control the conversation. To be an exceptional relationship manager you must also be an exceptional conversation manager.

There are five additional techniques I use in conversations that may seem elementary, but have been proven highly effective, simple to do and easy to implement:

1. Go slow: vary your pace

Slowing down can be an uncomfortable thing for the fast talkers of the world to do. Many relationship managers feel they need to talk fast and fill the space with words. They don't want to allow silence in the conversation because they're trying to impress their clients. If you're nervous, you'll tend to speed up. Filler words showing up is a good indication you're going too fast. Instead of stopping and giving yourself time to think, your motor mouth continues to run. Instead of deliberately and powerfully choosing your words, you rush. The car is moving but for those moments, no one is steering. Slow yourself down or at a minimum vary your speed.

2. Go low: vary your volume

Reducing the volume of your words at certain points in a conversation for effect is a powerful technique. Most train horns blast at 140 decibels, and a rock concert rocks your ears at 125 decibels. A normal conversion occurs at 60-70 decibels. A whisper is at 20. If you tend to speak on the louder side of things, lowering your volume as a contrast gives notice to the other person that the topic you're discussing is important. Or, if he hasn't been paying attention, the change in volume should draw him in.

3. Put down one card at a time: simplify

Separating complex concepts or messages into small bite-sized pieces is essential. Let's say you're explaining a rule change in your industry and how it's going to affect your client's account. The result of the change is he will need to open a new account. It's very inconvenient and a tough message to deliver. An example of chunking it down:

1. "The company decided to make a change…" [pause, let them hear what you just said.]

2. They did it in response to a new rule at XYZ Government Agency… [pause, let them absorb.]

3. Because of this decision, we're going to need to open a new account for you.

By chunking things down and pausing a tad longer than you may be comfortable with, he's naturally going to think, "And what will I need to do?" The result you want is for him to anticipate needing to do something rather than you telling him outright. In contrast, saying it all in one sentence that goes, "You need to move your account because there was a rule change" could surprise your client. You'll likely need to repeat yourself and provide further explanation. By putting your cards down one at a time, you make your message easier to receive.

4. Use your client's name: personalize

Dale Carnegie said, "*A person's name is to him or her the sweetest and most important sound in any language.*" Inserting his name strategically keeps him engaged. When he may have zoned out, saying his name will regain his attention. But, watch overusing or forcing his name into what you're saying. Use it a few times strategically and it will make him feel your communication is tailored especially for him.

5. Give it a rest: stop talking intentionally

The idea of the rest in music is an important one to consider. It's the break in the music that is juxtaposed against the sound. The ability to stop talking on a dime requires self-control. Inserting an intentionally long pause after asking an important question or making an important point will also add impact to your communication. Learn to become comfortable with pausing to maximize your impact.

Challenge yourself to use these five techniques: go slow, go low, deliver one concept at a time, use their name and give it a rest. You'll increase your effectiveness at important junctures in your conversations.

Conclusion

Approach each conversation with the idea that your behavior in the conversation will be decisive. Your ability to exercise self-control in your conversations with your client will determine how and where your relationship goes. A single conversation can be productive, fail to go anywhere, take the relationship backward or even end the relationship. The bottom line benefit of you successfully exercising self-control will be client loyalty. You will earn credibility as a skillful communicator because of how you conduct yourself. Think about the impression it makes when someone appears out-of-control and how poorly that reflects on him.

If you incorporate the lessons from the first five chapters of the book: build rapport, use questions skillfully, listen, focus on needs, and exercise self-control you'll be far ahead of most relationship managers who give little thought to any of these skills, domains or endeavors.

But you can't stop here. You need to be prepared and have a plan.

Lesson 6 • Prepare and Plan

HOW MUCH TIME do you put into preparing for a conversation with a client?

To add value in a conversation, it's important to distill, condense and refine your thinking such that the information you provide is useful and valuable. It's important to weed through the huge amount of information in the world, to understand the history, context, major events, and competitive landscape such that you can differentiate between what's noise and what's significant. The best way to ensure you deliver the most important takeaways and key points to your clients is to develop them in advance, not in the moment.

Early in my career, I didn't prepare much at all. I remember making one introductory phone call to a new client named Gary. I looked over Gary's application quickly and then dialed his number. He answered skeptically without even saying hello, "I checked you out online. People have written a lot of negative things about your company."

I hadn't anticipated this kind of start at all. I had envisioned a conversation where things would move forward simply because we were talking. But, I was totally wrong. Up to that point, this was the standard way I had approached conversations. My plan would be simply to get the conversation started and adjust from there. In this case, I wasn't afforded a chance to adjust. After less than a minute, he quickly said, "You know what, I've changed my mind. I'm not moving forward," and then he hung up.

The problem was I didn't have a plan for anything other than a cooperative new client. I expected I'd give an overview of the account opening process then field a few questions. I thought if he asked a question I didn't know the answer to, I would ask if I could get back to him. But, Gary didn't give me any such opportunity. I had gotten on the field without a game plan. No plan was the wrong plan. And because of my lack of preparation, my company lost out on tens of thousands of dollars of annual revenue.

My mentor, Mark, bluntly said to me, "I don't know why you think this, but you're not good enough to wing it." I was surprised and offended. I didn't think I was winging it. I thought I was good enough to improvise. But now, looking back, I can see I really wasn't. And after that one conversation with Gary, I decided I would never let something like that happen again. I decided I would have a plan for every single conversation.

What about you? Do you enter a conversation with a plan? Or, are you content to improvise and make things up as you go along? Many relationship managers are. If you want to be an average relationship manager, that's fine, but it's not if you want to be an excellent relationship manager. So, approach each conversation with a solid plan. Anticipate what can go wrong. If you don't have a detailed game plan for the entire conversation, then you haven't gone deep enough into the planning process.

Be Prepared by Having Talking Points

While you may be concerned you won't have enough to say, your clients are likely afraid you will talk too much. Talking in a long-winded fashion, or meandering and not making any points, may cause your clients to think:

a) He doesn't seem prepared.
b) I wish he would be more concise.
c) It seems like he's thinking out loud
d) He's wasting my time with long and hard to follow answers to my questions.

Avoid having your clients think any of these thoughts by being fully prepared.

One way to be prepared for your conversations is to write out talking points in advance. Talking points are your access to being concise and precise. They help you to be able to consistently offer value. I keep a list of talking points that I can pull up on my computer in less than 7 seconds so when I'm on the phone and I need to explain something complicated I don't have to go searching for facts, figures, concepts or distinctions. If I'm in a face-to-face meeting, and can't access my notes, I've at least thought through my points ahead of time which makes them more specific and impactful. The simple act of preparing talking points helps me to be more thoughtful when I'm answering questions or presenting information.

Talking points are not a script to read from, but rather than putting together thoughts on-the-fly, I can leverage the information I've already distilled and thought through ahead of time. This way I can focus on my delivery and on managing the conversation instead of having to focus on what I'm going to say next. I call this pre-talking—it's like being my own sous-chef for the conversation. All the different parts of the metaphorical meal I'm cooking are prepared ahead of time so that I can concentrate on putting all of the ingredients together instead of both preparing and cooking at the same time.

Being able to boil down complicated topics and concepts into 5, 10 or 15 second explanations is essential to getting your points across. It demonstrates that you're prepared and that you respect your client's time. Attention spans are short. Even a client who might appear to have a lot of extra time on his hands doesn't want to listen to long-winded speeches or run-on tangents. He wants sound bites and values a quick, clear and concise statement or response. After your initial short statement, he might prefer more, but he can always ask for it and you could always offer it. Starting with a short statement doesn't mean you can't elaborate from there.

When writing, it's easier to see that sentences or paragraphs are getting too long. But, when you haven't thought things through ahead of time, it's easy to slip into long run-on sentences. A stream of disconnected thoughts makes it hard for your client to follow you. Maybe you're excited or are thinking out loud. Maybe you're trying to make too many points or fit in too much content. If you tend to speak in run-on sentences, my advice is to think about inserting punctuation in your speaking, as if you were writing.

Your goal is to be concise. What people want from you as an expert is value, not a lot of words.

There's a fallacy that says the more you know, the more effective you'll be at your job. But it's not what you know, but how you demonstrate and apply what you know, that will determine your success. This takes planning and practice. It's quite easy for the rookie relationship manager to spout off technically correct details about his company's products or services that he learned in training while saying absolutely nothing that his client really wants to hear.

Long-winded talk, which can be full of details and words, can be incomplete and off the mark. Being eloquent means economizing your words.

We have experts all around us (and often need their expertise), but rather than wanting to have them tell us everything they know, we would prefer they formulate everything they know into concise information and advice. You could call this specialization of information and expertise. We live in an information age, but we don't necessarily need more information. I would say the greater risk is overload and overwhelm. Someone who can take tons of rock and extract the gold for us is highly prized. A message simplified into short bullet points saves us from getting lost in massive amounts of information (and misinformation).

Study and prepare to refine your talking points. Take the pages and pages, and books and books, of information you have on your product, service, industry and competitors and refine your message into bullets. Put in the time to read seriously with the intention of providing value in short phrases that highlight important concepts. In other words, create a depth of understanding such that you can give a concise yet complete answer. Having talking points means you're ready for a discussion. Your talking points are key plays in your playbook.

Develop a Repertoire

In addition to having talking points, it's helpful to have a good repertoire to artfully help you connect with your clients. A good repertoire consists of several short plug-and-play sequences that can be inserted into a conversation.

A good repertoire includes:

- Metaphors
- Analogies
- Short stories
- Examples
- Rhetorical questions
- Comparisons
- Distinctions
- Philosophy
- Quotes

Your repertoire will help you to simplify the complex and maximize efficiency. Dudley Field Malone said, *"One good analogy is worth three hours discussion."*

Metaphors that are made personal work best:

- medical metaphors for doctors
- construction metaphors for engineers
- art metaphors for artists
- sports metaphors for sport enthusiasts
- pet metaphors for pet lovers

If you can have a visual metaphor for a visual person you'll doubly enhance your effectiveness. Consider the value of auditory or kinesthetically related metaphors too.

If you can't find something relating to a person's profession, there are universal metaphors that work for everyone: driving in a car for example. While it's true not everyone drives, everyone will have ridden in a car or at the very least, seen one! Do people like to sit in the front seat or sit in the back? Do they prefer to drive or prefer to let someone else drive?

Eating is another good place to find metaphors. Of course, everyone eats; although you don't want to overfeed your client when a simple metaphor will satisfy his appetite. Operating in metaphors engages people in a conversation at both an experiential, logical and often interesting and fun level. It's a great way to simplify and quickly creates a shared understanding.

Stories are a very good way to make a point while also helping your clients relate to you. Comparing and contrasting different concepts will deepen understanding. Drawing distinctions by comparing your company with your competitor, or your product and services with another company's will help further your client's understanding.

In addition to metaphors and stories, analogies are good for concisely demonstrating logical thought. An analogy is a comparison between two things: A is to B as X is to Y. One of my favorite analogies in discussing different types of stock market declines is when I say a thunderstorm is to a hurricane as a correction is to a bear market. Analogies can communicate in a simple and complex manner at the same time.

Rhetorical questions (ones you aren't asking them to necessarily answer) can also make your points effectively. Some questions can address a frequent objection simply because there is only one logical answer. For example, when a client complains about fees, I'll ask: "What's more important: the amount of the fee or your return net of fees?" My point is made in my question. There's only one logical answer. It's like checkmate in one move.

Be clear about your overall philosophy. Being grounded in philosophy gives you something to fall back on when your conversation strays or you feel like you're standing on shaky ground. It creates a foundation for the expression of your ideas. When you depart from your core philosophy you aren't as powerful as when you adhere to it. For instance, when clients are myopically focused on the news of the day, I'll often share that I don't pay much attention to the news—that I find history and books to be much more helpful guides than short-term reactions and noise. The core philosophy is to think long-term. Or, I'll draw on a few select quotes to support my philosophy. For example, Harry Truman said, *"The only thing new in the world is the history you do not know."* Mark Twain quipped, *"History doesn't repeat itself, but it does rhyme."*

There are lots of tools in your talking toolkit, but unless you are intentional about which tool you're using, you'll likely grab the first one from the top of the box and it may not be the sharpest tool in your shed.

Follow a Structure

You might be thinking that putting a plan together for every single conversation sounds really time-consuming. Can you really take the time to plan for all of them?

The solution is to have a ready-made plan that you can adapt to every conversation. The best way to do that is to follow a structure. Having a structure to follow frees you up to manage the multitude of other elements you must consider in a conversation. You don't have to reinvent the wheel in every conversation. My recommendation is a needs-based model with four distinct parts. Each part has clear objectives and makes it easier for you to fulfill your purpose of satisfying your client's needs and deepening your relationship with him. A structure gives you a basic roadmap for your conversations.

I admit that years ago when the idea of a conversation structure was first introduced to me as part of a sales training program, the concept seemed unnatural and inflexible. I questioned, "How can I apply a single structure to every single conversation?" But, now that I've worked within the same structure for thousands of conversations, I see how it guides me skillfully through all types of conversations and situations. Practiced thousands of times, it's become mental muscle memory and I follow it almost automatically. I know if things aren't going well it's because I'm not following my plan.

Here's an introduction to the four parts of the structure I follow:

1. Create: To bring into existence

- Make an opening statement
- Establish rapport
- Gain agreement on objectives
- Determine what needs to be accomplished
- Listen (or check) for acceptance on the direction of the conversation

2. Explore: To inquire into or discuss a subject or issue in detail

- Probe and uncover information on needs, wants, motivations, and circumstances
- Obtain a clear and complete understanding
- Build consensus/agree on the needs and issues to be dealt with
- Listen (or check) for acceptance of your understanding

3. Address: To speak to (typically) in a formal way

- Present solutions that meet and satisfy your client's needs
- Discuss features and benefits on multiple levels
- Handle objections
- Listen (or check) for acceptance of proposed appropriate solutions

4. Resolve: To agree on solutions to problems and needs

- Understand how to deal with "no"
- Place yourself on the same side of the table
- Use the language of agreement to ask for a commitment to appropriate next steps including specific dates and times

The central themes that are woven throughout the structure:

1. You orient the conversation around your client's needs.
2. You gain agreement as you create, explore, address and resolve.
3. You listen or check for acceptance systematically before moving on to the next part.

This can be your mantra: uncover needs, gain agreement and check for acceptance. Note: you may need to explore and address many items before you can ultimately resolve the conversation.

An Example of a Needs-Based Structured Conversation

My goal is to call my client John to discuss his circumstances and needs. My objectives are to:

1. Ascertain his loyalty and evaluate if the relationship is at risk
2. Determine ways the relationship can be deepened
3. Discover opportunities to win additional business

I view this conversation as an opportunity to play both defense and offense.

Create

Ivan: "Hello John, it's Ivan calling. How are you?"

John: "I'm good. It's good to hear from you."

Ivan: "Great. It's good to be heard by you. The purpose of my call is to give you an update, address anything on your mind and see if you need anything." [This is my opening statement. It includes a purpose for calling and proposes a conversation that center around addressing his needs.]

John: "Okay. I can't think of anything I need right now, but I'm always open to an update." [At this point, there's no stated need, but he has accepted the premise and direction of the conversation.]

Before engaging in the actual business conversation, and depending on the level of rapport we have, I might take the time to discuss what's going on in his life. For example: "John before I give you an update, how have you been doing lately?"

Explore

Ivan: "There are many different things I can update you on. In order that my update is most meaningful to you, is there something you'd especially be interested in hearing about?"

John: "You know, come to think of it, I'm approaching retirement and I don't think I understand the best time to start taking social security." [Amazingly a need surfaced. I asked one closed-ended question and while a few minutes earlier he said he couldn't think of any needs, he thought of one. This happens routinely. Since human beings always have needs, given some amount of time and space, a client will usually come up with something.]

Ivan: "What do you already know about social security?" [Rather than launching into an explanation and providing details that may or may not be relevant, I start with an open-ended question.]

John: "Not much. I haven't really thought I'm going to get that much or that it's going to be a significant part of my retirement plan."

Ivan: "How much time do you have to discuss this? What level of detail would you like to go into?" [This helps to understand circumstances and assess style preferences.]

John: "I only have a few minutes right now, but it's worth going into the details in about a month from now."

Ivan: "So you do need to discuss it, but not right now. Correct?" [I just stated the need and checked for acceptance.]

John: "That's right."

Address

Ivan: "Since you only have a few minutes, may I make a couple of quick suggestions?" [Checking for acceptance (or asking for permission) that he's ready for me to speak to his needs.]

John: "Go ahead."

Ivan: "First off, we have a lot of resources to help you. Secondly, I'm going to suggest you do some homework in preparation for our next conversation."

John: "That's good to know, but what am I going to need to do?"

Ivan: "Well, in order to make this most impactful for you, I would suggest you contact the social security administration or go to their website and determine your actual benefit. It's pretty easy to do and I'd be glad to walk you through it over the phone." [When I address needs, I'm presenting possible solutions and addressing any potential objections.]

John: "Is it really that easy?" [Minor skepticism].

Ivan: "It can be if you know what you're doing. I have an idea."

John: "What is it?" [John has accepted that I'm going to propose a solution."]

Resolve

Ivan: "I suggest you check out the website before our next conversation, but if when I call you next month, you haven't gotten to it yet, we can do it together."

[I have put forth a specific suggestion for him to accept or decline. I made it pretty easy for him. I said he could either do what I'm suggesting on his own, or I'll do it with him. The goal is to satisfy his need of knowing this important information for planning purposes. Of course, the larger goal/need is to support him in building a complete financial plan in retirement. This becomes my map for my adding value over the years to come.]

John: "That sounds good to me. Thanks for calling." [John agreed with the proposal.]

Ivan: "What's the best day and time next month for me to follow up with you?"

John: "Two weeks from today would probably be the best day. I have the day off. I think sometime in the afternoon would be best."

Ivan: "Perfect. Why don't I call you around 2:30 PM?"

John: "That works for me." [We have agreement on a specific action at a specific time to address a specific need.]

Conclusion

My challenge to you is to make every conversation count by making sure you have a plan.

Think about how many substantial client conversations you may have in any given day. The number is likely in the single digits. By substantial, I mean conversations where you can express your leadership and value as a relationship manager by dealing with complex situations that require you to provide advice and deliver expertise. These are important opportunities to make a difference and key to developing the long-term relationships you seek to build with your clients. They require a level of depth to have maximum impact. Given that you'll have very few of these conversations every day—maybe you'll only have one—you have no excuse for not being prepared and having a plan. Moreover, keep in mind it's possible that you might talk with some of your clients only a once or twice a year. Therefore, to become an extraordinary relationship manager, you have to make every conversation count.

When you have a plan and a structure you are putting yourself in a position to effectively manage and lead a conversation. While some may feel like a structure is imposing and inflexible, having a structure guides you so you can in turn guide your client. I have faith in the model I use. More than 10,000 conversations have proven that beyond a shadow of a reasonable doubt structured conversations work.

A structure allows me to enter every conversation with the confidence I can focus on leading and managing the conversation instead of wondering, "Where am I and where do I take it from here?" Building rapport, using questions skillfully and listening are important, but unless you can fully address your clients' needs, you will not have achieved the most important element of your job which is to retain and grow client relationships. Be prepared and follow a structure. Doing so helps everything else fall into place.

$$\textbf{Create}$$

$$\downarrow$$

$$\rightarrow \textbf{Explore}$$

$$\textbf{Address} \leftarrow$$

$$\downarrow$$

$$\textbf{Resolve}$$

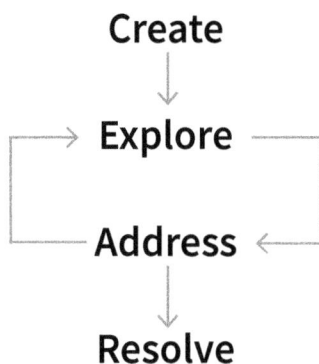

I acknowledge that there are countless structures that different authors, coaches and trainers offer. My point here isn't to say my model is the only one, my point is having a plan and following a structure is important. If you've got another structure that you're inclined to use, that's great. My recommendation is to pick one model and do thousands of repetitions with it until you become excellent at it and can do it subconsciously. Now, let's get into the first part of a conversation.

Lesson 7 · Create

HAVE YOU EVER jumped right into a conversation you're not ready to have? I have many times—too many times.

Most conversations are reactions to someone else's circumstances instead of being well thought out and set up to be successful. Some parts of a conversation count more than others. The opening part is one of them. Imagine the presidential candidate who flubs his opening statement in a nationally televised debate. The nation is watching carefully, and he just made a first impression that he'll struggle to recover from. Initial missteps are more difficult to overcome than conversations that get off to a strong start. You never get a second chance to make a first impression.

Imagine climbing into a swimming pool, positioning yourself in a spring position against the wall, and then propelling yourself off the wall. Now imagine causally easing into the pool and starting to swim from a position where you aren't touching the wall at all. It's not that you can't get moving but it takes more effort. Creating a conversation with a weak start is like starting to swim a without getting a good push off the wall. Eventually you'll get moving but it will take you longer to get where you want to go. The wall of the pool is a springboard for swimming with maximum velocity just like a strong start is a platform for an effective conversation. Put yourself in position to get a good push off the wall and set yourself up for success.

Make an Opening Statement

At the risk of being perceived as too formal, always prepare an agenda. I believe stating an agenda increases the probability that your clients feel that they're working with a professional and indicates you care about them and the outcome of the conversation. An agenda lays out the goals for the conversation. Most relationship managers underestimate the importance of setting an agenda as the foundation for an effective conversation. By setting an agenda in a positive and professional tone and starting with a specific consultative opener, you position yourself as an expert, a professional and a problem solver. Engaging in a consultative needs-based conversation necessitates getting the other person to buy into the process and to open up.

The words "reason" or "purpose" are important and valuable words to integrate early in your openers. "The reason I called is _____." or "The purpose of meeting with you today is _____." Never enter a conversation without a reason or purpose. If you don't determine the objectives, you run the risk of having an unproductive conversation.

When creating an agenda, keep a few basic questions in mind:

1. What are my objectives?
2. What might his objectives be?
3. What needs to be accomplished?
4. What are the important items we need to discuss?
5. If there is a project involved, what are the next steps?

There are numerous benefits of declaring an agenda:

- You show you gave thought to the conversation in advance.
- You provide the reasons for the conversation and give your client the opportunity to determine if he wants to proceed with this conversation at this time.
- You create a pathway to achieve goals and objectives in your relationship with him.
- It helps you to be proactive.

How many items should be on your agenda? My answer is three. I suggest a three-part agenda is best because it chunks things down, is less overwhelming but still occurs—and is—meaningful and substantial.

You may have 46 items you need to cover with your client, but if you start with "I have a long list of agenda items," it's overwhelming and could create resistance instead of buy-in. You can always add items to the agenda once in progress when it seems natural and/or the clients take you in that direction.

Three seems to be the maximum that clients can handle when they are deciding whether this sounds like a conversation they want to have with you. Three is a magic number.

Agenda Example:

The purpose for our meeting is threefold:

1. Give you an update on some changes you need to know about,
2. Get an update from you on your situation, goals and needs, and
3. Address anything else that is on your mind.

There are accounting terms used in cost accounting and inventory measurement called LIFO and FIFO. (LIFO is an acronym for last in first out and FIFO stands for first in first out.)

It continues to surprise me, but happens predictably, that whatever I state as the third item in my three-part agenda is where the conversation generally starts. It's almost as if they didn't hear the first or second item on the agenda. The recency effect causes us to hear the last item in a list more than the other items. Unless you intentionally go back to the first item (declaring your agenda as First In First Out), the conversation will likely start with the third item you mentioned. So, while it may seem counterintuitive, I typically list the item I want to start with in the third position. In the example above, my goal was to find out what he was thinking about first so I intentionally listed that last.

Envision how you want the conversation to go. To shape your vision and plan, there are many reflective and planful questions you can ask yourself:

- What am I committed to?

- What are my intentions and goals?

- What needs to happen in this conversation?

- What are the ways I can add value?

- What kinds of questions could I ask him (and why)?

- Am I fully prepared to say what needs to be said?" (If XYZ topic comes up, have I thought through the important points?)

- Where do I want to take the conversation?

- If it were to go well, what would the result(s) of the conversation be?

- How do I think he's going to respond to what is said and what might my responses be?

- How can I make this conversation valuable for him?

- How can I create a good mood and positive tone in this conversation?

Asking these kinds of questions will help you create a meaningful conversation. In my experience, when most relationship managers approach a conversation by thinking about the topic or topics, they ask themselves things like, "What do I want to talk about?" or "What am I going to say?" A different way to approach a conversation is to ask yourself the above list of questions before you begin. Envision how you want the conversation to go and remember to orient yourself toward your client's needs.

The first part of the conversation is important. When a client begins to engage in a conversation with you he consciously or subconsciously asks himself, "Will this be pleasant or unpleasant, productive or unproductive, useful or a waste of my time?" If he thinks it will be pleasant and productive it increases his willingness to give you his time. As a relationship manager you'll signal your competence from the start when you make a powerful opening statement.

Read the Defense

What separates the best quarterbacks in football from the average or rookie quarterbacks is their ability to quickly and accurately read the defense by looking at how the defense is lined up and what happens as the ball is snapped. If you're going to create a strong conversation, you'll need to be able to read your clients like an elite quarterback reads the defense.

Have you ever picked up the phone and even if you haven't spoken with your client for months, it's like you never stopped talking with him? Or, have you ever talked with a client just a few minutes earlier, but when you return to him the conversation is awkward and stilted and whatever rapport you had at the end of the last conversation has vanished? An important part of reading the defense in a conversation is monitoring the level of rapport. While you'll need the skill of reading the defense throughout the entire game it's especially crucial at the start. You must make sure you know what the defense has in store for you in every conversation if you're going to execute your plan effectively.

Over time, I've been able to hone my ability to read my clients. Getting a client talking early and often in a conversation is key. Since I know I'm going to ask a lot of questions, the first thing I do is assess how open and willing the other person is to respond to my questions. It's especially important to get a new client talking. There could be someone who's been your client for years and has become very predictable. However, in each conversation, you still must read and discern what the defense is doing now. You never know what a person is bringing to a conversation on any given day. (His dog might have just died, his father might have been diagnosed with cancer, or he may have just learned he's becoming a grandparent for the first time.) You may recall from Chapter One on rapport that I recommended going beyond saying "How are you?" to your client by asking three rapport questions. This is certainly the time to do so.

There are other aspects of reading the defense. As I noted before, if asked a closed-ended question, it's unlikely a client will give you much more than a one word yes or no answer because that's what a closed-ended question asks for. Some clients will simply not give you a lot to read. Most will go further and may modify, qualify or even discount their answer, but you can note what questions are helping the conversation progress and where a closed-ended question is causing it to stall.

When I ask an open-ended question, is his answer: short or long, confusing or clear, vague or ambivalent, simple or complex? What is he exhibiting about his communication style and preferences? What are the most important things to him? Do I sense any reluctance or discomfort?

One of the benefits of the rapport sandwich that I discussed in Chapter One is it gives you the opportunity to read your client before you delve into the meat of the discussion. A client's willingness to answer questions before you discuss the agenda items tells you how easy or difficult it's going to be to collaborate with him in the conversation.

For example, let's say I'm entering a conversation where I fear my client might end his relationship with my company. My goal is to find that out as soon as I can in the conversation so I can know how to proceed. But in that situation, I would very rarely start by saying, "My goal today is to determine and assess your loyalty and interest in remaining our client." because that would likely be perceived as too direct. Also, it makes it all about me and my needs.

A simple opening statement like, "My objective is to give you an update and address anything on your mind." is designed to find out exactly what he's thinking or feeling. One of the ways to read whether your relationship is in jeopardy is to see how much he'll answer. A client who may be ending a relationship with you will begin to shut down communication. He'll make it harder and harder to get a read on him—he's increasing his defenses.

Rookie relationship managers often have a more difficult time reading the defense than veterans do. Things move too fast for them and they're not as skilled at knowing all the potential challenges and obstacles they'll face. But when veteran relationship managers stop paying enough attention to the defense, they limit their effectiveness and may get caught off guard.

Use a Consultative Opener

In order to discover what your client is seeking to accomplish, your opener must get your client to open up. A good consultative opening statement includes a short declaration and a question inviting them to talk.

Here is an example:

"I am fully prepared to discuss your relationship with our company and address any questions you may have. What would you like to accomplish?"

Consider a few benefits of this kind of statement and question:

- You provide assurance and confidence he's dealing with a prepared professional.

- You're able to assess your client's willingness to share/open up and tell you what's on his mind and what his goals are.

- You indicate to your client you're going to be attentive to what they want to accomplish.

Here are some other examples of opening sentences:

- "The purpose of this discussion is to provide you with some information, but before I do that, please tell me if there's anything you'd like to make sure we discuss."

- "I have a number of things on my list to discuss with you, but before we go over my list, would you like to tell me what's on your list?"

- "The reason for this meeting is I need some information from you, but before I ask you some questions, I want to make sure I understand what might you need from me."

Many openers end with a question, but it also works if you make a clear statement that you need and value his input and will make addressing his needs an important part of the conversation. If you do this consistently, your client learns you're going to start by asking him what he needs. You'll find he becomes more prepared to tell you what he needs from you. It creates the basis for a relationship where you are focused on his needs and he's fully aware of that from the start.

Most of the time a relationship manager will respond immediately to the first thing the client says, but I've found the first part of your client's answer is not typically what he truly wants to talk about or even what's most important. Be committed to listening and waiting. If you're patient and disciplined, what typically happens next is he'll share more. He may list off a second, third, fourth item on his mind as if he were unpacking a suitcase. The most important stuff is often at the bottom and comes out last. As he gives you an answer, he becomes clearer about what he wants and needs. By being patient at the outset of the conversation, you increase the likelihood you'll find out what he really wants to talk about instead of guessing. It's much more impactful and useful to obtain this information in the first few minutes of the conversation rather than leaving it up to chance for happening sometime in the conversation—or maybe not ever happening at all.

Typically, relationship managers are so ready, willing and eager to discuss their products, services or updates that they skip over finding out what the client wants to discuss. Relationship managers have spent a lot of time training to be experts and learn about the features and benefits of the products they represent. Rookies seem especially eager to display whatever new knowledge they possess. It is as if they feel like they will be successful only if they pass a knowledge test. In their minds, they get points for providing information but leave the client thinking "How long am I going to have to listen? When are we going to start talking about me and my needs? This may be interesting information, but it has nothing to do with what I need."

Little things matter in conversations. Using consultative openers at the start of a conversation is more important than displaying what you know as soon as you can. Find out what's on their agenda. As Steven Covey advocated, *"Seek first to understand before being understood."*

Check for Acceptance

Check for acceptance of your opening statement. It could be your client doesn't accept it at all—and that's fine. It allows you to create the agenda with him and get his buy-in from the start. Additionally, one way to check for acceptance of your agenda is to ask if there is anything he'd like to add to the agenda. When you do, you confirm that you haven't missed anything, and you get clarity on the direction of the conversation. You're both headed toward the same destination, which is key.

You can check for acceptance in three main ways:

1. Ask a short opened-ended question:

- What do you think?
- How do you feel?
- What's your opinion?

2. Ask a closed-ended question:

- Does that make sense?
- Do you get what I mean?
- Do you see what I'm saying?
- Are you okay with _____?
- Do you agree?
- Is there anything you would like to add?

3. Be silent. Pausing longer than you might normally invites your client to fill the silence with his feedback and/or acceptance.

An intentionally long pause may feel a little uncomfortable at first, but it's crucial to let him think and consider what he wants. Often times, he'll respond with a statement like, "Well, that's a good question." because it buys him time. This allows for you to check for acceptance of your opening statement. It could be your client doesn't accept it at all and that's okay because you want to know whether or not you have buy-in from the start. If he doesn't accept it, you're better off knowing.

While there may or may not be acceptance for what you've put forth, you can only know when you check and get a response. Face-to-face you could be observing body language (i.e. head nods), but in conversations over the phone you have no such opportunity, which is why you need to ask directly.

Conclusion

I used to think I could follow the cliché advice: fake it until you make it. But that was before I worked with my mentor, Mark. I thought I was a good conversationalist and could coast through the start of every conversation, but Mark would always let me know when he caught me being unprepared. If I were going to be the professional I was committed to being—and be excellent in conversations—it meant I needed to plan every conversation beginning with a powerful opening statement.

A commitment to excellence in conversations means having a plan for every conversation and getting a strong start by intentionally creating it. Most people don't realize how unprepared they are because it is so incredibly common to enter a conversation without a plan, a purpose, or an agenda. A strong start is easy to achieve with preparation and planning. There's no excuse for being unprepared. Legendary football coach for the San Francisco 49ers (1980-1987), Bill Walsh, had his first 15 plays planned and practiced all week before every game. Focus on the first 15 seconds of your conversations and it will make a big difference.

Lesson 8 · Explore

HAVE YOU EVER BEEN involved in a conversation that you thought was going well, but it actually wasn't? Suddenly, your client gets frustrated and blurts out, "You don't understand!"

Perplexed, you later analyze each part of the conversation and still can't understand why the conversation didn't go well. The fact is, you may have heard the words he said but you didn't fully explore what he meant. In order to dig down for the good (and bad) stuff and discover the many sides of every need and story, you need to have tools to do so.

Most relationship managers assume they know what their client's needs are, but generally their understanding is far too superficial and assumptive. To engage in conversations that have true depth you must work to understand needs beyond a superficial level. When done effectively your relationships are strengthened. Usually, relationship managers focus on the tip of the iceberg, but the kind of depth I am talking about is the part of the iceberg under the water or maybe even underneath the iceberg itself!

I believe that the main reason a client leaves you is because you've not fully understood his needs. If you fail to understand his needs then you'll fail to completely satisfy his needs and he'll have no choice but to find someone who will. As a relationship manager, you cannot have a reasonable basis for offering solutions to your clients when you don't have a clear and complete understanding of their needs. Exploring effectively relies on many of the skills we've discussed previously in the book: a good rapport, the skillful use of questions, listening well and exercising self-control.

Use Questions to Probe

When I use the word "probe" I am talking about using a question to uncover valuable information, and to explore and examine a set of needs and circumstances such that you'll be able to provide a resolution.

Clarifying and understanding the full nature of your client's needs helps you to become aware of any potential problems. You can't get a complete understanding without probing. Moreover, after many years of probing effectively, I don't see how someone could truly be an effective relationship manager without probing skillfully. Effective probes encourage a client to talk about his personal opinions and feelings, think critically and make good decisions.

Asking follow-up questions is essential when you do not fully understand a response to one of your questions or one of your client's statements. In the great majority of situations, a simple probe like "What do you mean by that?" will help make your conversation more productive. The absence of follow-up questions leads to a surface level discussion and leaves you guessing or assuming what your client means. Many of your client's statements will be vague, ambiguous or undeveloped. Words are often spoken before critical thinking has taken place. How many people do you know who start talking without thinking through what they're going to say?

You can tell when your client hasn't thought through what he's said because when you restate or paraphrase what you just heard, he looks at you in disbelief, "Did I really just say that?" Many times, upon being asked to clarify, your client may quickly realize what he's just said either isn't completely true or is something he doesn't believe and didn't really mean. Try it out. Ask someone to tell you what he meant and see how his story changes.

Successful Probing: Probing is successful when there is a clear, complete and mutual understanding. What I witness consistently is most understandings are vague, unclear, only a small part of the story and based on false assumptions. In some ways, probing is like mining for gold. You must be patient, dig deep and sort through a lot of rock to finally confirm that you've gotten the gold.

Relationship managers consistently move forward on top of an incorrect and inadequate understanding. They may think they have a clear and complete understanding, but truly don't because they haven't fully explored. Both you and your client may think your understanding is clear and complete, but what appears clear to one person may not be clear for another. Also, you may feel you have a complete understanding, but it may be completely wrong, which is why checking for acceptance to determine if you share the same understanding is so important. Your goal in probing is to create a clear, complete and mutual understanding of the situation, circumstances, wants, needs, thoughts and motivations.

Being an extraordinary relationship manager means being extraordinary at probing. A mantra I repeat to myself when I am probing is: clear, complete and mutual; clear, complete and mutual; clear, complete and mutual.

For example:

Clear	Client: "I need to save money." Ivan: "What do you mean?" Client: "I don't think I can afford your fees anymore." Ivan: "What makes you say that?" Client: "I'm having trouble keeping my cash reserves at a level that I feel comfortable with." Ivan: "Thanks for sharing that with me. I'm now clear why you're uncomfortable."
Complete	Ivan: "Is there anything else I should know?" Client: "Yes, my spouse is concerned as well. We'd like to know if you'd be willing to reduce your fees?" Ivan: "I see." Client: "We'd like to stay with you but feel like we can't." Ivan: "Please tell me more." Client: "Well we haven't looked for a less expensive alternative, but we're going to in the next month or so." Ivan: "I appreciate you telling me that."
Mutual	Ivan: "So, what I heard is the fees you're paying make it difficult to keep your cash reserves at a level where you feel comfortable. As a result, you think you need to find another place do business even though you'd prefer to stay with us?" Client: "That's correct."

Become Skilled with Different Types of Probes

Previously, in Chapter Two, we discussed when to use the two major types of questions (open-ended and closed-ended) in conversations. While correctly using the right question type will make a huge difference for you, in this chapter we'll go beyond using open-ended and closed-ended questions as generic tools and move into a discussion of several specific probes you can use to explore, manage and lead conversations. After asking thousands of questions, I've discovered many valuable uses for them.

Metaphorically speaking, an open-ended question is like a crowbar. You can use a crowbar to open a window, but you wouldn't use a crowbar to open someone's chest to perform open-heart surgery; you'd use a razor-sharp scalpel. Similarly, a closed-ended question is like a hammer. You can use it to nail things down but after performing brain surgery you wouldn't use it to stitch someone's skull back together.

In this next section, I'm going to present several concepts based on the two major types of questions and will be using the word "probe" synonymously and interchangeably with the word "question." In other words, I'll be calling open-ended questions "open probes" or closed-ended questions "closed probes." In some cases, to further abbreviate, I'll identify them simply as "open" or "closed."

While it's true most people don't ask enough questions, asking more poorly designed or poorly timed questions won't help you to be more effective. It's not the number of questions that makes your probing effective, it's the skill in knowing when and how to strategically use the right probe.

Open-Ended Probing Concepts

1. Leads

Leads are open-ended questions designed to set, change or direct a segment within the conversation. They are called leads because they lead to the next topic in the conversation.

Generic examples:

- What do you think about _____?
- How do you feel about _____?

Specific examples:

- What do you think about the recent changes we made in your portfolio? [leads to discussing the changes]
- How do you feel about the stock market right now? [leads to discussing the stock market]
- What's your opinion about the future? [leads to talking about the future]
- Looking back, how do you think things went? [leads to an evaluation]

Depending on your tone, leads can be used in a relaxed and non-threatening fashion or you can turn up the pressure a bit almost throwing it back at them. "How do you think it went?" could be said with many different tones. Leads allow you to control and lead the conversation. Leads are easy to ask and unexpectedly powerful. They can help you steer conversations or shift the focus. If a conversation drifts where you don't want it to go, you can bring it back on track with a lead.

2. Assessors

Assessors are probes designed to help you assess your client's mindset or his level of knowledge on a specific subject. Before discussing a topic or answering a question from your client, you can determine how to handle the question by asking questions: "How familiar are you with _____?" or "What do you already know about _____?"

When your client asks you about a specific topic (i.e. bonds, inflation or account types) you can respond with something like:

- How familiar are you with bonds?
- What do you already know about bonds?
- What's your experience been with bonds?
- What's your understanding of how bonds work?
- What's your definition of inflation?
- How much do you already know about the account types we offer?

Use assessors to make sure you're headed down the right path. A relationship manager might get far into an explanation before realizing he's telling his client something he already knows, or his answer is completely over (or under) his client's head. Asking: "What do you already know about _____?" can save you time and avoid a situation where your client feels you're being condescending because you're telling him things he already knows. Assessors also help you gauge the level of complexity with which you need to handle the information you provide your client.

3. Motivators

Motivators are used when you want to understand someone's motivations:

Generic examples:

- How does that affect you?
- What is the impact of that?
- What prompted you to say/ask that?

Too often we'll guess why a client asked a question and begin to answer it from our assumption as to why. Much like with assessor probes, it makes sense to understand the motivation behind their statement or questions.

Examples:

- What prompted you to ask that question?
- How does _____ affect you?
- What makes you say _____?
- What motivates you to _____?
- How do you feel your current plan will impact you down the road?
- What led you to ask about your account's _____?

Motivator probes help you understand what's important to your client and what drives him. If you ask him an open-ended question about his goals (for example, "What are your goals?") he may answer it by telling you, "My goal is to make a lot of money," "Climb the corporate ladder," or "Do a lot of good in the world." Motivator probes can be used to understand what will cause your client to make changes and how to make an offer or solution compelling to him. You can't rely on what motivates you or other people, you must specifically know what motivates him.

4. Clarifiers

A clarifying probe is used to clarify the meaning of the statement and further the understanding you have of what your client said.

Generic examples:

- What do you mean by that?
- Help me understand what you mean.
- How did you come to that conclusion?
- How come?
- How so?

Specific examples:

- What did you mean when you said our service is _____?
- Help me understand what you mean when you say something is _____.
- How did you determine that you need _____ in order to get _____?

Most of the time, asking your question will help you to address a question and understand the true need(s). It reduces assumptions. While making assumptions can save you time, it can take you down the wrong path, be a diversion and unintentionally prevent you from truly understanding.

5. Continuers

A continuer is a short question or phrase designed to encourage your client to keep talking and elaborate. As an added benefit, they will help you listen better. Continuers are a core component of active listening as we discussed in Chapter Three. Continuers help clients feel heard and allow you to obtain additional valuable information that you might miss if you were to interrupt them or stop them after the first part of their answer.

Examples:

- Tell me more.
- Go on.
- And then?
- Really?
- What else?

Many times, a relationship manager stops a client after the first part of his answer. He hears the answer he was looking for and will move on. Or, he'll hear a different answer than what he wanted (or expected) to hear but still move on. In both cases he could simply ask the client to continue. It takes discipline to do this, but it's worth it for the valuable information you'll get. Your client needs time to fully express himself. Encouraging him to continue will be rewarding. Moreover, when he is upset and wants to tell you about it, a combination of motivator probes and continuers can be a powerful way to peel back the many layers and complexity of his feelings.

6. The W Questions

A journalist is taught to cover the story with the Ws: who, what, when, where and why. Keep the Ws in mind as a good reminder that to get a clear and complete understanding of a situation, we may need to come at it from a number of different directions.

Examples:

- Who is the money for?
- What kind of cash flow needs will you have in retirement?
- When do you plan to retire?
- Where do you plan to retire?
- Why did you choose to work with us?

You can count on the W questions to obtain important information so you can present specific products, services or solutions in a relevant fashion. It's all too common for a relationship manager, working from assumptions, to have already decided what he's going to present even before he has all the facts. Using the W questions is a good support structure for being consultative.

7. Greasers

Sometimes conversations need some "grease" to get them moving. Either your client is generally quiet and reflective or for whatever reason doesn't feel comfortable in the current situation/conversation. Before trying to engage in a discussion he's uncomfortable with, you need to find a way (or ways) to get him moving. Getting him to answer any question at all sets the gears in motion for additional questions.

Examples:

- What do you think about the weather?
- What's your hometown known for?
- What are your hobbies or interests?
- What is the origin of your name?

Greasers help a conversation flow and build rapport. When you're getting to know your client and learning how to most effectively talk with him, getting in a rhythm of asking and receiving answers to your questions is important. Start with a topic he knows a lot about, thereby greasing the wheels of progress in the conversation.

8. Hypotheticals

Hypotheticals are probes directed to a future decision. A well-phrased hypothetical probe is what gets you a reading on the eventual decision without explicitly asking for the decision. It also indicates that a decision-making conversation is coming. Asking a hypothetical ensures you're headed toward a no-surprises proposal. "If you were to _____, how would you make the decision?" Asking about his decision-making process makes it into a "pre-decision" conversation. You're telegraphing your intentions in a way that is both indirect and direct at the same time. Using the word "if" allows you an opportunity to make your probe hypothetical.

Examples:

- If you were to replace your current car, what type of car would you be looking for?

- If you were to decide to retire, what would you need to have in place?

- If I were to ask you to consolidate all your different accounts at our company, how would you feel?

- If you had to tell your other providers you're leaving them for us, what would you say?

- If you were to make a change in your long-term strategy, what kinds of things might you use in your decision-making process?

The words "if any" can be used to turn a closed-ended question into an open-ended question:

- "Do you have any questions?" can become: "What, if any, questions do you have?"

- "Do you have any reservations?" can become: "What, if any, reservations do you have?"

9. Sub-decisions

A sub-decision is a decision leading up to a larger decision. Sub-decision probes can also be hypothetical in nature. There's less pressure in making a series of small decisions versus one large one. Some clients have a lot of anxiety around making decisions, especially important and complex ones. You can really help your client make large decisions by making lots of little ones along the way. This reduces the risk of making a mistake and helps your client to be more comfortable. He doesn't have to make the larger decision, he just needs to consider one part of it.

Examples: (two choice or multiple choice)

- For your next car, would you prefer it be red or blue?
- If we were to meet next week, would Thursday or Friday be better for you?
- When you open an account will you fund it with cash, check or wire?

Single choice sub-decisions are closed-ended probes:

- Would you like your next car to be red?
- Do you want to meet next Friday?
- Do you plan to investigate your pension plan before the end of the year?

Sub-decision probes can be either open or closed and you'll probably use a combination of both. The open one with two or more choices is narrowing the focus. The single choice nails down the specifics.

Before we move on to closed-ended concepts, here's a reminder from earlier in the book.

Open-ended questions are best used to:

1. Generate dialogue
2. Direct the conversation and forward the action
3. Elicit facts, feelings, motivations, needs and wants

Closed-ended Probing Concepts

1. Confirms

Confirms are needed throughout your conversations and are a frequently used and useful tool. You can use them to confirm your understanding, confirm your client is getting what he needs, confirm he agrees or disagrees with you and/or confirm your understanding of what he means.

Examples:

- Do you know what I mean?

- Do you hear what I'm saying?

- Does that make sense?

- Do I understand you correctly?

- Is that okay with you?

- Are you ready for us to move on?

- Are we in agreement?

To stay in sync with your client, use confirms throughout a conversation. They're the main way to check for acceptance and gain agreement. They're also an important part of active listening and collaborating. When you know that what you've discussed has been accepted before moving on, you've built a foundation for additional agreement. Confirms are the best way to learn you've successfully (or unsuccessfully) probed because only by asking, can you find out if your understanding is clear, complete and mutual.

Moreover, when making assertions to a client, it's easy to assume what you've put forth was accepted if he didn't dispute it. But later when you ask yourself, "Did he actually accept what I said or just didn't react?" the answer is often: "I don't really know." Your client may have voiced his fear of the stock market going down and you gave logical reasons why he shouldn't be afraid, but do you really know if you changed his mind if you didn't confirm it? It's best to confirm before moving on.

2. Engagers/Hooks

Engaging questions are a certain type of confirming question used to make sure your client is actively involved in the conversation and he hasn't drifted off or tuned you out. Especially in situations where you have a lot of information to cover, you want to make sure he is still listening. I also refer to these question types as "hooks." Your goal in using a "hook" is to catch him on your metaphorical fish hook and start "reeling him in." The hook is a question used to get a reaction and involve your client.

Examples:

- Are you with me?
- Do you get where I'm going?
- Do you see what I mean?
- You get that, right?
- Do you have an opinion about it?
- Are we headed in the right direction?

Engagers can also be used as a quick pause. Engagers are by design closed-ended because you're truly not inviting a client to elaborate or respond beyond a yes or no answer. If you really wanted to give him the floor instead of asking, "Do you have an opinion about _____?" you'd make it open-ended and ask, "What is your opinion about _____?" If you sense you're losing your client's attention, then you always have the option to switch your engagers to an open-ended question thereby ensuring he will re-engage because he'll be the one talking. As we discussed previously, this is a surefire way to get someone to pay attention.

Finding the right balance of check points with engagers can help both of you. Perhaps the client likes what you're talking about and how much you're talking, but perhaps you're talking so much he's disengaged. Engagers help you to know if you're beating the same drum. Stopping periodically to see if he's fully connected to the conversation can be very useful. This is especially true in phone conversations when you cannot see affirming or disconfirming head nods.

3. Isolators

Isolating probes can be used through the conversation and help determine if you're able to move forward.

- When setting the agenda:
  » Is there anything else you want to make sure we talk about?
- When discussing needs:
  » Is there anything else you need me to know?
  » Is there anything I missed?

- When receiving objections:
  - » Is there anything else you're skeptical about?
- In determining next steps:
  - » Is there anything else we should consider before we determine next steps?

Isolators are used to unpack all the things on your client's mind. If he is upset, make sure to give him the opportunity to vent. In addition to listening, a well-timed, "Anything else?" can help make sure he has identified all the issues causing him to be upset. Often, when a client is upset, it may be about several things. If you try to address each one as they come up instead of isolating and determining that there aren't any remaining issues, he'll likely be distracted by the fact that he still has communication he needs to deliver. It's possible there's only one issue to cover, but if there's more than one, by interrupting him you've prevented him from fully unloading which may cause him to become more upset.

Lastly, isolators are a great tool to use to end/close a conversation, such as, "We've covered everything on my list. Is there anything else you need to cover?" Once you've given your client a chance to answer and his answer is, "There isn't anything else I need right now," you can respond by letting him know you'll be available if there is. "Let me know if you need anything else." is a great way to end a needs-based conversation. You've discussed his needs and opened the door for future discussion and support in meeting his needs.

4. Interjectors

Interjectors are questions that offer a way to stop the action. They provide an acceptable way to interrupt—and not be perceived as rude. (People will commonly say, "I don't mean to interrupt, but..." when they most assuredly do mean to interrupt because they just did.) Instead, you can use a question.

Examples:

- May I interrupt you for a moment?
- May I ask you a question?
- Can I add some additional context before you continue?
- Do you mind if I interject?
- Can we take a step back for a moment?

Getting permission with an interjector is preferable to interrupting without asking, but you must be careful not to overuse them. Save them for important points in the conversation when it's clear your client misunderstands something that is important for you to promptly correct.

For example, if he says, "Your fees are very high and because of that I'm moving my business elsewhere." you could respond with an isolator as in, "Are there any other reasons?" A timely interjector can buy time and allow you to probe further.

5. Helping Verb Inquiries

The most common and basic closed-ended question types—the ones that seem to be asked automatically—use verbs that modify other verbs. Core helping verbs are forms of be, do or have.

My purpose for bringing up helping verbs as a question type is to point out that the great majority of questions people ask start with helping verbs. The way these types of verbs are used can at the same time be too specific and/or too blunt as tools.

Examples:

- Do you see how this product will work for you?
- Are you satisfied with our services?
- Did you enjoy the seminar?
- Will you be opening another account?
- Have you ever recommended our company to others?

"Did you have a good weekend?" forces someone to say yes or no. It lacks a certain freedom for them to elaborate and may quickly cut off the interchange. People answer questions such as "Did you have a good _____?" reflexively without giving much thought. Changing your question from a closed-ended one to an open-ended one will change the nature of your conversations. "How was your weekend?" leads the responder to say, "It was ____" and will likely share additional information. Asking "Did you have a good weekend?" logically leads to "I did. Did you?" Both parties in the conversation checked off a box but have not set the stage for an opening act.

The helping verb questions are the antithesis of the W questions; they force a "yes" or "no" answer, whereas Ws invite a fuller richer response and gather facts, feelings, motivations, needs and wants. Nailing things down and checking for acceptance are the best times for helping verb probes.

By way of review, closed-ended questions:

1. Request a quick answer

2. Check for acceptance of what you've put forward

3. Determine if you've obtained agreement

4. Make a statement or point

Summary of question types:

Open-ended	Closed-ended
1. Leads	1. Confirms
2. Assessors	2. Engagers/Hooks
3. Motivator	3. Isolators
4. Clarifiers	4. Interjectors
5. Continuers	5. Helping verbs
6. The W Questions	
7. Greasers	
8. Hypotheticals	
9. Sub-decisions	

Conclusion

If you've probed successfully, you and your client have clear, complete and mutual understanding of your client's needs.

In most conversations the needs are assumed because not enough follow-up questions are asked. A relationship manager proceeds without clarifying what his client meant when he made a statement. Adjectives go unchecked. The client's thesis goes unquestioned. The relationship manager avoids stating the truth: "I'm not clear what you mean by that." He doesn't question the motivation behind the statement by asking, "What led you to say that?" or "How did you come to that point of view?"

Asking clarifying questions leads to completeness. Ask follow-up questions and take the time to understand the issues, stories or concerns from many different angles.

If you don't have time to get complete information, you can make a statement: "While we might not have enough time right now to get to the bottom of this, I need to make sure I fully understand your concern before I can properly address it. When can we get deeper into this?"

Use your active listening skills. Remember to paraphrase and restate. "I heard you say that your expectations were unmet, and you're upset because what you thought was going to happen, didn't occur. Am I correct?" When you ask a closed-ended confirm such as, "Am I correct?" and he responds affirmatively, you've succeeded in creating a clear, complete and mutual understanding. It's how you know you can proceed.

Ultimately, it's the depth and closeness of the relationship that make the biggest difference toward success in retaining and growing your client relationships. When you can help your clients understand their needs you will be providing an uncommon service. Clients look to you for your leadership. Depth of discovery makes you closer to them. The word intimacy can also be thought of as into-me-see. Intimate relationships require a high degree of trust. You will truly be an extraordinary relationship manager if you can build the trust necessary to delve deep.

An added benefit of using all these different question techniques and probes is it also allows you to manage the flow of a conversation.

Probing successfully helps you add value. Once you have a clear, complete and mutual understanding you can proceed to the next phase: addressing needs and handling objections.

Lesson 9 · Address

HAVE YOU EVER FELT like you're putting in a lot of effort to get your client to use your company's services correctly? You've told him how things are supposed to work. You've explained and presented your products, but again and again he comes up with reasons why he doesn't want them or need them. You think you know exactly what he needs, but he dismisses your recommendations like a customer at a restaurant sending his food back to the kitchen.

As a relationship manager, you need to know how to leverage what your company offers in order to satisfy the needs of your clients and solve their problems. It's at the core of how you add value for both your client and your company. However, most relationship managers focus on becoming proficient at discussing the details of their company's offering from the company's point of view rather than from the point of view of how it addresses their client's needs. Also, while knowing how to discuss your company's offer is important, being able to address your client's needs and objections is equally as important as the solution itself.

Objections are a normal and expected part of how a client responds to your presentations so you must know how to effectively handle them. Your role exists because sales brochures and websites can't talk through the products and services with clients and handle objections like you can. When you provide information and explain what your clients should buy from you, you should expect them to respond with varying degrees of resistance from hardly any to complete defiance. Encountering resistance is normal and should be expected—not resisted by you in return. Handling resistance effectively is an important part of successful relationship management.

Many relationship managers go wrong by:

- Reacting to objections in a counterproductive fashion
- Mishandling objections and invalidating their clients' feelings
- Battling instead of acting consultatively
- Improvising instead of following a process for handling objections

By responding in a less than optimal way, they increase resistance and create unnecessary conflict. Instead of presenting and then defending, present and then expect to deal with objections. When you anticipate and even welcome resistance, and have a plan for dealing with it, you can enter every conversation expecting a positive outcome. Psychologist Carl Jung suggested that what you resist not only persists but grows in size. Learn how to handle your client's resistance properly and it will go away, not be in the way.

Clearly Present Features and Benefits

The reason why you explore needs before addressing them is because the best time to present products and services to your client is after you have a clear, complete and mutual understanding of his needs. At that time, you have a better chance of having him accept the solutions you present. Your presentation needs to show how your company's solutions will meet/satisfy his needs.

While there are many ways to present, I would recommend:

1. Introduce the product or service
2. Give a brief description of it
3. Highlight the most relevant and important features
4. State the benefits related to those features.

What are features and benefits?

- A feature is a single characteristic, attribute or aspect of your product or service.
- A benefit is the advantage gained from a feature.

A majority of relationship managers don't set the context for introducing their products and services in a clear, simple and logical way. They fail to describe the important and relevant features clearly even though they have lots of product knowledge. They act like a waiter who reads the entire menu to the customer instead of highlighting one or two items on the menu.

In general, relationship managers aren't encouraged to keep their presentations simple. But, presentations that are full of unnecessary information are unproductive. Moreover, if you describe features but don't link the features to benefits (and needs) then all you've given him is a description of features, not what's in it for him. Helping him understand how he'll benefit increases the likelihood he'll accept what you've put forth.

When you're presenting complex products, it can work well if you present one feature at a time and check for acceptance before moving on to the next feature. This breaks things down, makes it easy for him to digest the information you're providing and avoids overwhelming him. You may know your products inside out, but it's probably new information for him. An added benefit of presenting one feature at a time is that it will help you to isolate what (if anything) he objects to. With simple products you may be able to list a few more features at one time. Note: you also don't need to list every feature possible because that overcomplicates things.

Example:

Let's say you're a relationship manager for a bank and your bank offers three different types of checking accounts: Basic Checking, Premier Checking and Ultimate Checking. You present the checking account types to your client and highlight a few aspects of each, "The basic checking includes five checks a month without a fee." You pause and observe whether he accepts it as something he wants or declines it as something he doesn't. The feature described is five checks a month and the benefit is the account is free if your client stays within the limit of five checks.

Let's say he doesn't accept it because he needs to write more than five checks. You continue, "The Premier checking account offers 20 checks a month with no fee if you set up a direct deposit of your paycheck. This way you'll get more checks and not have to come into the branch every week to make a deposit." You pause to determine if he accepts the features and benefits. He says, "20 checks are sufficient and not having to wait in line every month would be good." The feature is the ability to write 20 checks and the benefit is he has a sufficient number of checks in order to pay his bills. The second feature is direct deposit and the benefit is he doesn't have to wait in line to deposit his checks.

Lastly, you contrast the first two products with the third one, "Ultimate Checking includes unlimited checks, an interest-bearing account and reduced rates on mortgages if you set up direct deposit and have two or more accounts with us."

If you had started your conversation with an agreed upon agenda and probed first for needs, then you could simply match the product with their needs. In addition, you could state the features and benefits that meet the needs for which you've already gotten mutual agreement for.

A conversation might go as follows:

You: "What would you like to accomplish today?"

Client: "I'd like to open a checking account."

You: "Is there anything else you need?"

Client: "No that's it."

[You have a clear agenda and therefore can proceed.]

You: "What are you looking for in a checking account?"

Client: "I need to write 10-15 checks a month and have direct deposit."

Now it becomes clear to you that the client needs your Premier Checking account. You may still present all three types of accounts to compare and contrast the different features and benefits to make sure to create the best fit for your client. Your client likes to be offered at least two choices, but three is optimal. Psychologically, this allows him to sort out and try on different choices and helps him feel like what he's getting is the best one. Without a comparison it can feel like one product is pushed. Having choices helps him to see you as a consultant. Note: you didn't need to discuss other unrelated features (for example, statements, the number of branches the bank has, 24/7 telephone customer service or online access). Isolating the features and benefits that most relate to the needs you've surfaced in probing is key. If another need is surfaced while you're discussing features and benefits, you'll probe about it and then present additional features and benefits.

Discuss Solutions on Multiple Levels

While you need to be proficient with your company's offer and how it stacks up against your competitors, you must also think beyond features and product knowledge. You must be able to connect relevant features directly to benefits and to how they satisfy your client's needs.

For example, an investment representative may focus on his company's past track record rather than what the investments can do to support his client's needs (such as investing to generate enough cash flow for the rest of his life). So, you could say, one benefit of having your investments managed by XYZ company could be the creation of cash flow. But the cash flow may not be the ultimate end. The need for cash flow could also be the need for comfort, confidence or peace of mind.

Another example: a car salesman may focus on the engine type (it has eight cylinders) or how fast the car can go (from 0 to 60 miles per hour in four seconds flat), but those are features. He needs to check with the customer to see what's most important to him.

Listening for your client's needs, anticipating them and helping to surface them through a consultative needs-based conversation is powerful. By having a needs-based conversation versus a topics-based conversation it becomes completely clear that the value being provided aligns with the value that is needed. A question such as, "What do you need most from the car you're looking to purchase?" would be a good way for the salesman to get the customer thinking about his needs. The salesman may be looking to sell a car for its prestige, but the customer may simply need dependable transportation and isn't interested in prestige at all.

As a relationship manager, it's also important to think creatively about what you offer. What separates you from other relationship managers is being ready and able to discuss your company's offer as it relates to your client's needs. I view this discussion as being able to operate within five distinct levels:

Level One	Features	You're prepared to articulate and highlight all the features of your company's products and services.
Level Two	Benefits	You're prepared to connect and point out many benefits to each of the specific features.
Level Three	Needs	You're able to state how a feature benefits your client and meets, supports or satisfies his specific needs.
Level Four	Needs Underneath Needs	You can create awareness of the need underneath the need.
Level Five	Basic Human Needs	You're able to understand and empathize with your client's basic human needs. I refer to this as operating in the realm of the need underneath the need underneath the need. Ultimately this is about relating at a human level and helping your client achieve their core needs.

Here are a few examples to illustrate what I mean so you can map out the five levels when preparing for a conversation:

Example: A Mutual Fund

Level One—Feature: 10-year track record

Level Two—Benefit: The managers are experienced

Level Three—Need: Long-term return and growth

Level Four—Deeper Need: Peace of Mind

Level Five—Human Need: Safety

Example: A Phone Plan

Level One—Feature: Unlimited texts

Level Two—Benefit: You don't have to pay for each text you send

Level Three—Need: Saves money/allows you to text more

Level Four—Deeper Need: Staying in touch with all your friends

Level Five—Human Need: Belonging/Affiliation

Example: A Bank Account

Level One—Feature: Bill Pay

Level Two—Benefit: You can pay your bills without having to write checks

Level Three—Need: Saves time and money paying for stamps

Level Four—Deeper Need: Makes you more organized

Level Five—Human Need: Self-efficacy and self-esteem

Going beyond features and benefits helps you to empathize and relate to your client. It personalizes the discussion of your company's offer and connects it to your client's needs at a deeper level. By focusing on needs with empathy and connection you can go from simple to profound.

When I orient myself around how my company satisfies my client's needs on many levels, I feel I am making a difference rather than selling. I feel I'm helping my client get what he needs in his life to fulfill his goals and dreams. I'm on a journey with him on the path to self-actualization. It becomes a mission versus a business transaction.

Relationship managers rarely think beyond features, and hardly ever talk about or specifically point out benefits, so if you do, you're ahead of most. Go three levels deeper and you're operating underneath the iceberg.

Have a Process for Handling the Four Types of Objections

Even when the products you have to offer are an exact fit for your client's needs, it's incredibly rare that you'll present them and the client will simply say "yes." Done, conversation over. Resistance and objections arise because things rarely line up perfectly.

Because receiving objections is inevitable, what you need is a process for handling them so when you get one or more objections—which will be most of the time—you'll know exactly what to do and be able to handle them methodically and professionally.

How you react to resistance and objections is very important. It's all too easy (and typical) for you to make your client's resistance mean your presentation wasn't effective or he doesn't like or trust you. Instead of making resistance or an objection mean something about you, step aside like a matador facing a charging bull, and depersonalize the discussion of the product or service. Your client is very unlikely to be objecting to you personally. Moreover, he is likely objecting to his own assumptions about and interpretations of the products and services you presented—not the presentation itself.

You'll have a better chance of handling objections if you know what they are and have a plan for each one. The four major types of objections are:

Skepticism	Your client doubts a feature or a benefit you've described and therefore feels you can't fully meet his needs.
Misunderstanding	Your client thinks you can't or don't offer a feature or benefit you truly can and therefore doesn't know you can fully meet his needs.
Drawback	Your client is dissatisfied with the absence or presence of a feature or benefit which makes him feel his needs can't be fully satisfied. One or more features are desired but not available, or one or more features are present but undesired.
Indifference	Your client is satisfied. He doesn't have any needs at this time and feels all his needs are met. You offer products and services that can satisfy his needs, but he is indifferent to discussing his needs. He accepts the status quo.

To illustrate this, here are some examples of what you might hear from your clients to indicate the types of objections they may have:

Selecting a checking account:

- Skepticism: "I doubt it's really free checking. There must be hidden fees."
- Misunderstanding: "I want the Ultimate Checking but I also want to set up direct deposit."
- Drawback: "I want to be able to come into the branch and you said it's only free checking if I set up direct deposit and don't use the branch."
- Indifference: "I'm happy with my current bank. The products seem just as good as yours."

Purchasing technology consulting services:

- Skepticism: "I doubt the credentials of your consultants."
- Misunderstanding: "I didn't know you provided consulting."
- Drawback: "I see you provide consulting, but we already have an in-house consulting group," or "You sell hardware, but I wish you also provided consulting services."
- Indifference: "Our current technology is working well for us. I don't need to learn about your services."

Buying a mutual fund:

- Skepticism: "I'm not sure about a fund with such a short track record."
- Misunderstanding: "I want a mutual fund, but I want to be able to set up a periodic distribution and you don't offer that."
- Drawback: "I don't want to own a fund that has only been around for less than two years."
- Indifference: "I think my current mutual fund is fine."

Deciding whether or not to have elective surgery:

- Skepticism: "The surgery seems expensive. Will it really make a big difference for me?

- Misunderstanding: "You don't offer anesthesia."

- Drawback: "You don't provide follow-up therapy and I wish you did."

- Indifference: "I don't think I really need this surgery. I'll live with the inconvenience."

The process for handling each of the four types of objections has many similarities and a few subtle but important differences.

Similarities:

- Acknowledging and/or naming the objection

- Asking for permission to learn more/ask questions/probe

- Using an abundance of questions

- Listening actively, clarifying and re-stating

- Addressing the specific objection

- Checking for acceptance and confirming your understanding

Differences:

- To address skepticism, you also must present relevant proof to build/rebuild credibility.

- To clear up a misunderstanding, you must provide an explanation and additional context.

- To overcome a drawback, you must shift the focus to the big picture and other agreed upon benefits.

- To deal with indifference, you must create an awareness of drawbacks to the status quo (motivation away from) as well as opportunities for change (motivation toward).

Address Skepticism

	What you do	Examples of what you might say
Step 1	Acknowledge and name it	"It sounds like you're skeptical." "I'm hearing some skepticism, am I correct?"
Step 2	Ask for permission to learn more	"May I ask you a few questions?"
Step 3	Probe, discover and learn where their skepticism is coming from	"What makes you skeptical?" "Where did your skepticism come from?" "Please tell me more about your point of view."
Step 4	Listen actively and clarify to get a clear, complete and mutual understanding of their skepticism	"So what you're saying is in the past because we didn't do _____, you don't think we'll be able to do_____ in the future. Is that correct?"
Step 5	Ask for permission to address their skepticism	"May I address your understanding?" "May I respond to provide you with some additional information/clarification?"
Step 6	Offer proof and build credibility	" I understand why you are skeptical, here's another way to look it." "You're right that we don't offer _____, but here are three things we do offer."
Step 7	Check for acceptance	"Now that I've given you an explanation, are you still skeptical?" "Have I fully and completely addressed your skepticism?" "Now, do you feel we can meet your needs?" "What are your thoughts at this point?"

Address Skepticism Example:

In this example, a prospective client responded to a direct mail solicitation.

> Todd: I've never heard of your company before. No one I know does business with you.

> Ivan: It sounds like you're skeptical.

> Todd: Yes, I am.

> Ivan: May I ask you about that?

> Todd: Okay.

> Ivan: What do you already know about us?

> Todd: I know that I got something in the mail from you, but you don't have an office near me.

> Ivan: So, if we had an office near you, you might feel like we were in your area and other people you know might have done business with us as well.

> Todd: That's correct.

> Ivan: So other people doing business with us is something that would build our credibility with you?

> Todd: That's right.

> Ivan: May I address your point of view?

> Todd: Go ahead.

> Ivan: While we don't have a location in your area, we do have a relationship with the police department, fire department and post office—all in your area.

> Todd: Really?

> Ivan: Yes, and not just that, we also do work for the city.

> Todd: I didn't realize that.

> Ivan: Now that I've provided this information to you, are you ready to talk further about you doing business with us?

> Todd: Yes, let's go ahead.

Clear Up Misunderstandings

	What you do	Examples of what you might say
Step 1	Acknowledge and name it	"I think there may be a misunderstanding." "I think you might be seeing it differently than we do."
Step 2	Ask for permission to learn more	"May I ask you a few questions?"
Step 3	Probe to learn more about what they understand and what they do not understand	"What exactly is your understanding?"
Step 4	Listen actively, clarify and restate	"So, what I hear you saying is, you think _____. Is that correct?"
Step 5	Ask for permission to provide additional context	"Would it be okay if I explain how it actually works?" "May I provide you with some additional information?"
Step 6	Present information and provide an explanation to correct the misunderstanding	"How it actually works is _____." "What we actually do is _____." "When we say we _____, it means _____."
Step 7	Check for acceptance	"Do you and I now have the same understanding?" "Have I made myself clear?" "Have I clarified to your satisfaction?" "What's your understanding now?"

Clear Up Misunderstandings Example:

I was talking with one of my long-term clients named Barbara. She placed tremendous trust in my company and wanted to give us additional business in an area in which she didn't think we could help.

Barbara: I wish you did more than just sell banking products, I wish you also sold insurance.

Ivan: I think there might be a misunderstanding, may I ask why you think we don't sell insurance?

Barbara: Sure, go ahead.

Ivan: Where did you learn we don't sell insurance?

Barbara: I read your brochure and I didn't see anything about it.

Ivan: What was the color of the brochure?

Barbara: Green.

Ivan: The reason I ask is because our green brochure is our banking brochure.

Barbara: Oh?

Ivan: May I provide some additional context?

Barbara: Sure.

Ivan: Government regulators require we separate our banking and insurance divisions. This means when we're offering banking services we use the green brochure and when we're offering insurance services we use a red brochure. Does that make sense?

Barbara: Yes, it does.

Ivan: Would you like a copy of the red brochure as well?

Barbara: Yes, I would and thank you for clearing up the misunderstanding.

Overcome Drawbacks

	What you do	Examples of what you might say
Step 1	Acknowledge and name the absence or presence	"You think _____ is missing." "You think _____ shouldn't be here?"
Step 2	Ask for permission to learn more	"May I ask you a few questions?"
Step 3	Probe to understand why the presence or absence of a feature is an issue for them	"How does our not offering _____ impact you?" "What is it about _____ that affects you?"
Step 4	Listen actively, clarify and restate	"I heard you say you think _____ service is missing and should be available. Correct?" "You're annoyed that _____ is happening because it shouldn't be. Is that right?"
Step 5	Acknowledge/name the drawback	"I see that's a drawback for you."
Step 6	Present information such that you refocus on the bigger picture and other agreed upon benefits	"Even though we can't offer you _____, we can offer A, B and C. I think you agreed those were things you wanted."
Step 7	Check for acceptance	"Does the fact that we offer A, B and C, overcome the drawback for you?"

Overcome a Drawbacks Example:

I worked with a client named Steve who despite the fact that my company couldn't give tax advice, wanted to ask his question and get advice anyway:

Steve: Can you give me some tax advice?

Ivan: Unfortunately, no. We're not tax advisors.

Steve: Well that is unfortunate. I may have to find a company that does.

Ivan: Sounds like you feel strongly.

Steve: Yes, I do.

Ivan: You think we should give tax advice in addition to investment advice?

Steve: Correct.

Ivan: May I ask you a few questions?

Steve: Okay.

Ivan: How does our not offering tax advice impact you?

Steve: I feel like my financial advice is uncoordinated and that I'm going to make a mistake.

Ivan: What else?

Steve: I feel like you should be set up to do everything. Frankly I'm frustrated you're not.

Ivan: I see. [Long pause] So, what I hear you saying is you're frustrated and you fear if your investment advice and your tax advice aren't provided by the same company, that a mistake might happen?

Steve: That's correct.

Ivan: I guess we have a drawback. You want us to offer something we don't.

Steve: That's right.

Ivan: You've mentioned to me before that you like our location, our hours and our accessibility. Moreover, you've been pleased with our advice. Is that all correct?

Steve: That's all true.

Ivan: Well, even though we don't provide tax advice, we do offer all the things you like about us and we are willing to work very closely with your tax advisor. Our job is to help you avoid making investment mistakes and his job is to do the same with your taxes. We do this often and it works out quite well for our clients.

Steve: I hear you.

Ivan: So, will that work for you? Does that way of thinking overcome the drawback?

Steve: Yes, it does. [If it doesn't it might be because there is also skepticism or a misunderstanding you'll have to deal with.]

Ivan: Great.

Deal with Indifference

	What you do	Examples of what you might say
Step 1	Acknowledge their satisfaction with their current situation	"It sounds like you're satisfied with your current circumstances."
Step 2	Probe and learn about their current circumstances. (Because you're unlikely to get permission with indifference, you don't ask for it, you just jump right in with open-ended questions.)	"What do you like about your current circumstances?" "What makes you satisfied with your current provider?" "What are the pros of working with them?"
Step 3	Listen actively, clarify and restate their current benefits	"So, what you like about your current provider is _____. Correct?"
Step 4	Ask for permission to learn more	"May I ask you a few more questions?"
Step 5	Probe as deep as you can to create uncertainty, doubt and awareness of drawbacks. (Open-ended probes are important in dealing with indifference.)	"What if any drawbacks are there?" "What are the cons of what you're currently doing?" "Where do you see room for improvement?"
Step 6	Present examples to create an awareness of opportunities and consequences	"Other people like you have taken advantage of _____ and got the following benefits." "Like you, others were satisfied with their current provider until they learned _____."
Step 7	Check for willingness to learn more	"Would you like to learn more?"

Deal with Indifference Example:

I was reaching out to a client named Michael who had been with our company about a year. I had trouble getting a read on his satisfaction with our company. I couldn't tell how he was feeling about us.

> Ivan: I'm calling to see if you'd like to hear an update of our current outlook.
>
> Michael: That's okay. I don't need one; I read your newsletter.
>
> Ivan: Great. I'm glad you read it, it sounds like you're satisfied with it.
>
> Michael: Yes, I am.
>
> Ivan: What do you like about it?
>
> Michael: I'm just more of a visual person. I like the graphs and the charts.
>
> Ivan: So, because you're a visual person and like the graphs and charts, reading about our outlook is preferable to hearing it?
>
> Michael: That's right.
>
> Ivan: May I ask you a few questions?
>
> Michael: Okay.
>
> Ivan: What are the cons of reading it versus discussing it with me?
>
> Michael: Well, sometimes I do have questions and other times the charts are confusing to me.
>
> Ivan: What else?
>
> Michael: Sometimes I disagree with something you've written and would like to give you feedback.
>
> Ivan: Other clients have voiced the same thing to me. They also prefer to read instead of just hear our outlook, but they found it worked best if they read the report first, wrote notes on it and then scheduled a quick conversation with me. That way, they could both ask their questions and also provide me with their feedback. Would that work for you?
>
> Michael: Yes, it would.

Avoid Common Mistakes

Here are some common mistakes people make that are worth avoiding when you're handling objections:

1. Jumping to present solutions to your clients without understanding their needs

A common habit is when a relationship manager jumps into presenting products and solutions without first agreeing on his client's needs. Why waste time if he thinks he already knows the solution before the client opens his mouth or has a chance to explain what he needs?

2. Leading with "you should"

In addition to presenting solutions before a relationship manager has fully understood a client's needs, he may also jump right in to providing advice. Watch how often the word "should" comes spontaneously out of your mouth: "Here's what you should do," or "You know what you should do." It comes from a limited view of the world—your own view—and falls out of your mouth before your brain has thought about where you are in a conversation and if this is the right time to present a solution. Avoid leading with "should" because it gives the meaning something is wrong. For example, "You should start exercising" delivers a message that you're wrong for not exercising. Instead, "After discussing your needs, it's become clear to me that you may need to change your behavior. What do you think you need to do?" When he responds, "I need to start exercising," he's much more likely to start doing it because he's the one who came to that conclusion.

3. Guessing or assuming the client knows how he feels or what he needs

A relationship manager can easily and automatically read into the smallest of indications and jump to conclusions about what it means. A client will shift uneasily in his chair and he might interpret it as he is uncomfortable with how the conversation is going, when it might mean that he has a sore back. He'll see his client sweating and guess the decision-making process is being difficult for him so he'll decide to back off only to later learn that the client had a fever.

Most relationship managers spend all day guessing how people feel and assuming what they need. Use open-ended probes and frequently ask:

- "What do you think about _____?"
- "How do you feel about _____?"
- "What do you know about _____?"
- "What do you need?"

As I mentioned in Chapter Two, use open-ended questions as a way to engage your client in a powerful, needs-based and consultative conversation. Open-ended questions that are between three and seven words are the best. If you find yourself asking a longer question, consider you might also be making a statement. When you do this your client responds without really knowing whether to answer the question or interpret your statement inside of the question. Do what you can to edit yourself so your questions are short, concise and powerful.

4. Not fully hearing your client's point of view

In their eagerness to help and share what they know, a lot of relationship managers start talking before their client has finished. They mistake a pause for an opportunity to jump in or they might not even wait for a pause. Watch how much you and your colleagues interrupt. I catch myself frequently interrupting. It takes tremendous self-control to stop yourself from interrupting.

5. Overestimating your client's resistance

Each relationship manager may react in a slightly different way when encountering resistance from a client. Some may get defensive, some nervous and some will lose hope. Others will get frustrated, intimidated, fearful or resigned. But the major issue causing relationship managers to have such adverse and disproportionate reactions is they have not properly assessed the level of the client's resistance. Maybe the client has consistently given the same reason for saying no and you assume he's digging in his heels and is never going to say yes. I've seen people say "no" to something for well over a decade before eventually saying "yes." The key is knowing whatever you resist about what they resist causes their resistance to persist.

6. Underestimating your client's resistance

I've also observed countless times where a relationship manager completely underestimated and failed to anticipate the level of his client's resistance and he continued to press until well into the conversation when the client started growing increasingly upset. Show self-control and use probes to gauge the level of your client's resistance so you can respond accordingly. This is an important part of the seven-step method I presented earlier in this chapter. Asking for permission to learn more about his objections helps you to assess the level of resistance. It gives him the opportunity to choose whether he's going to resist you fully or open up and discuss where his resistance is coming from. If you give him space to voice his thoughts and feelings, he will likely relax and open up. Once you name or acknowledge an objection you can even ask how strong his objection is. For example, "I hear you're skeptical. On a scale of one to ten, how skeptical are you?" or "It seems to me that you've expressed some doubt. How doubtful would you say you are?"

7. Not asking for permission to probe

Many good questions are mistimed and undermined because they're asked prematurely. Even a good question will be ineffective when your client isn't ready for it and hasn't yet given you permission to probe. I'm not saying you need to ask permission to ask a question before every question, but as I've outlined in the above, there are certain junctures in a conversation to check and say, "May I ask you about that?" A good time would be when you're sensing resistance or when they seem to be shutting down, disengaging or becoming indifferent. He may say "no" when you ask if you can ask about something. It's important to find out why. The inclination is to move on; however, if you remain silent, a lot of the time he'll go on to provide an explanation about why he doesn't want to be asked about it.

8. Mistaking skepticism for mistrusting

A relationship manager will frequently hear healthy skepticism and turn it into a bigger deal than it is. He may even make an allegation, "You don't trust us, do you?" This is a mistake. Giving your client the opportunity to voice his skepticism is healthy. How you listen to him and handle his skepticism is key. Your client wants to be able to share his doubts with you. He sees it as your role to establish credibility of your company's offer. If you respond like he doesn't trust you personally, he'll likely pick up on that and you may create mistrust where none existed. Become very comfortable with skepticism and embrace your role in handling it. This will engender trust.

9. Blaming them for misunderstanding

Clients feel bad when they learn they've misunderstood something. Relationship managers frequently tell their clients they're not following the rules. They may state they believe the customer is always right, but not act like it and not show enough empathy for clients misusing their products. "You don't understand." comes across much differently than "There seems to be a misunderstanding." Take responsibility with phrases like: "I must not have been clear enough." or "I could do a better job explaining this." Your job as a relationship manager is to operate at whatever level your client is at. Learn about his current understanding instead of blaming him and making him wrong for it.

10. Invalidating the experience of a drawback

Clients often want and need something that your company doesn't offer and will be dissatisfied by the absence. You will add insult to injury if you invalidate their wish for something that isn't a part of your offer. Discussing drawbacks is difficult for relationship managers because they also wish they didn't exist, so they tend to apologize unnecessarily or make excuses: "I'm sorry we don't offer that" or "We can't offer that because _____." By probing you can learn about your client's experience and why he is experiencing a drawback. This will validate his experience and help him to feel you respect him. When you invalidate your client's experience, it's instinctual for him to also feel personally invalidated.

11. Accepting indifference

Accepting indifference is a fundamental error. The easy path is to move on quickly when they may say, "I'm satisfied. I don't need anything," but resist the temptation to do so. When a client becomes complacent about talking with you it's a warning sign. I've found that even after 10 years of working with a client, I can still find new ways to add value and new ways to strengthen and deepen the relationship and so can you. When you focus on addressing your client's needs on multiple levels you realize your job is never done. Everyone has needs and when they dismiss conversations with you by saying, "I'm happy. You don't need to worry about me," be wary about accepting that at face value. They may be brushing you aside on their way to leaving you for your competitor. Create awareness of opportunities and elevate drawbacks and costs of the status quo.

12. Not checking for acceptance

Have you ever gotten to the end of a conversation and you're looking back at it and think you did a wonderful job? You made lots of good points, and the client seemed to accept them well. But how do you really know? It's normal (and easy) to forget to find out if your client accepted your points. Maybe he didn't say anything to the contrary, but not disagreeing is not the same as agreeing. Check for acceptance of your ideas, presentations and proposals. Throughout a conversation check for acceptance for the direction of the conversation itself.

Offer the Dessert Tray

I adopted one my favorite strategies from watching what successful waiters do when offering dessert. There are a few different ways I've seen waiters ask for the dessert order:

1. Did you save room for dessert?
2. Are we having dessert tonight?
3. Would you like to see the dessert menu?
4. Would you like to see the dessert tray?

The phrase I like best is: "Would you like to see the dessert tray?" because a picture is worth a thousand words and a well put together dessert tray is going to increase the likelihood of closing the deal. So, I call the strategy I'm introducing here the "dessert tray" and feel it greatly increases the likelihood that my client accepts the way I address his needs and objections.

For example, when one of my clients asked me if he should be fearful of the stock market being high, my response was, "What prompted you to ask?" Then after listening carefully, I restated, "Here's what I hear you saying. Is that correct?" Next, I said, "Would you like me to address your concerns?" I've found that when I let my client decide he wants me to address something, it makes him much more receptive to my input, advice and opinions.

Conclusion

Handling your client's objections skillfully cements your role as a value-added relationship manager. Working through objections creates clarity and provides an opportunity for him to fully consider solutions to his problems and needs. It sets the stage for satisfaction. Exploring makes sure you understand his objectives before you try to handle them. If you haven't probed sufficiently, you'll find rapport will disappear. Handling objections well requires many of the skills we've discussed already: using questions skillfully, listening, focusing on needs and exercising self-control. Moreover, when value is clearly perceived, objections will begin to go away. Objections are like a mirage in the desert. Once you get close to them, they disappear.

Proceeding in a consultative fashion and seeking to look at things from your client's point of view is powerfully different than coming from a sales orientation and only your company's point of view. Although you do need to consider your company's needs, your clients don't need to. Your ability to put yourself in their shoes will create better results.

Resistance and inertia are powerful forces and require a catalyst to overcome them.

You are the catalyst. Conversations with you help your clients fully understand how features and benefits relate to satisfying their needs. They're necessary to overcome resistance or inertia. How you deal with resistance is an important part of how you provide value. If you can skillfully and effectively handle and overcome objections, you set the stage for success in what we'll discuss in the next chapter: resolving a conversation and gaining agreement for action.

Lesson 10 · Resolve and Gain Agreement for Action

WHEN YOU MAKE a proposal to a client, sometimes you'll hear "yes" and sometimes you'll hear "no." How do you feel about hearing "no" from a client? Is it a word you like to hear? Do you avoid a conversation because you're afraid your client might say "no" to you?

We don't like to hear the word "no." Think about how hearing the word "no" from your parents made you feel when you were a child. "No" probably made you feel bad or like you did something wrong. Children hear "no" a lot. Parents need to set limits: "No, you can't do that, that's dangerous. No, you can't stay up all night. No, you can't jump off that 12-foot high wall. No. No. No."

Even though "no" is just a word, it's still one of the most powerful ones. "No" usually prevents us—at least temporarily—from achieving our objectives. It's easy to give up and not want to ask again. The fear of hearing "no" inhibits us from powerfully and freely expressing ourselves and asking for what we want.

How do you feel about hearing "yes" from your clients? Is "yes" a word you like to hear? The answer is emphatically, yes. "Yes" means agreement. "Yes" makes anything possible. What could you accomplish if you were to hear "yes" more frequently from your clients?

Your ability to get a "yes" for action from your client is the best measure of your effectiveness and can be seen directly in the results you get—the results most important to a relationship manager: client loyalty and satisfaction, strong retention measures, and significant additional business. Remember your client's decision to continue or to increase his business with you results in real revenue and profit. The more business you generate the more it will make you valued by and valuable for your company. Gaining agreement for positive and productive action is essential.

Key thesis: The relationship you have with your client is the total of all the conversations you've had with him. It's all the words, thoughts, feelings, needs and motivations communicated and actions taken. The meaning of your conversations are the specific results—the next steps—that result from them. No matter how wonderful your conversations are, it's action that matters. Each conversation results in an increase, decrease or no change in the depth of relationship.

If you follow the outline recommended in this book, by the point in a conversation when it's time to resolve the conversation and ask for action, you've already agreed on the conversation's objectives and had a clear and complete conversation about your client's needs. You've presented and discussed potential solutions to address his needs and handled all his objections. Doing all this sets the stage for agreeing upon next steps: a clear and specific action plan with an agreed upon timeline for completion.

Proficiency in gaining and maintaining agreement with your client matters because it's the reason why you have a job. Client's feelings and decisions can be fleeting. A new client who recently decided to work with you can change his mind and tell you, "I'm having second thoughts." Or someone who has been with your company for years may one day wake up and say, "I think I need to make a change." One time, a client told me he had to make a change because he had Attention Deficit Disorder (ADD) and couldn't stay with any one company for very long. He said he got bored.

Gaining agreement for action means you'll get a return on your efforts. A conversation without any action coming out of it is like a waiter discussing the menu with you, but never serving you a meal.

Understand "No" is a Natural Response

Understand "no" from his point of view. In addition to you not liking to hear the word "no," your client doesn't enjoy saying it to you because he knows how it feels on the other side. You may have noticed he has a lot of trouble telling you "no." He may feel uncomfortable when asked directly for an answer and may even be upset with you for putting him on the spot. It's likely he won't want to disappoint you.

Asking for a decision changes the dynamics of a conversation and can make you and your client anxious. Your client doesn't want to be perceived negatively by you and when you ask him to commit to something, you are putting him in that situation. The tension of having to avoid saying "no" places a strain on rapport. Whereas a few moments ago you may have been speculating creatively about the many potential paths he could take, now you're asking him to decide on one (or more) of them. And deciding what path (or paths) to take also means deciding what path (or paths) not to take. This awkwardness leads to an avoidance of asking for a decision.

Asking someone to choose also changes the dynamics of a conversation. When someone has the space to choose, it means he's not being forced, pushed or cajoled into a certain direction. He doesn't feel manipulated, he feels he is voluntarily moving forward and actively pulling next steps and a new future toward himself. Even if he chooses what you want him to choose, he's not choosing it because you want him to—he's choosing it because he wants to. If he wants what you want, you have a mutual want and that creates alignment and collaboration.

Metaphorically speaking, the part of a conversation when you are seeking a resolution is like being in the red zone in football (inside the 20-yard line and looking to score). You've driven the length of the field, but getting into the end zone is different. The defense changes and has an incremental advantage. They can use the sidelines as additional defenders. The space is smaller. The importance is greater. And, so it goes with conversations. When you move for commitment (for him to commit money, time and/or physical or emotional resources) his defenses tend to become activated or reactivated. Being in a situation where he is required to make a decision brings up aspects that heretofore may not have been part of the conversation.

In addition to an uneasy relationship with saying "no," your client is also afraid to say "yes." He's afraid he'll regret his decision. Many questions will come into his mind. Even though you've already handled his objections, they can resurface when it's decision time. Your goal is to help support him psychologically. You do this by empathizing, and helping him voice the questions he likely voices to himself.

Examples:

- "What if I make the wrong decision?"
- "What if I regret the decision?"
- "Will I feel like I wasted my money or time?"
- "Will I really use the service?"
- "Will it be a good experience?"
- "Will I get what I paid for?"
- "Will it cause me problems or unintended consequences?"
- "What will other people think?"

And so on...

Because people both avoid regret and avoid saying "no," they find all sorts of different ways to say "no" without directly saying it. For example: "Let me get back to you. Let me think about it. I need to talk with my spouse first. Let me look at my calendar. Once I get my ducks in a row. I'm going to be out of town for a while, I'll make a decision when I get back…" Additionally, you may find they stop returning your calls and/or are suddenly unavailable to meet with you. The reality is anything besides "yes" is a "no." Or, at the very least, it's a "not yes at this time." A relationship manager often thinks a client has said "yes" to something because he hasn't explicitly said "no" to something. But, the real measure of a yes is when you have clearly agreed upon next steps and scheduled actions.

A Bad Feeling in His Bones

Some clients simply need more time to decide than others. I was assigned a technology professional named Max who told me he had a bad feeling in his bones. He said, "There's going to be a crash worse than any we've ever seen before. When the fit hits the shan, I want to be ready." In addition to keeping the majority of his money in cash, he purchased gold and silver bullion, several guns, built huge stockpiles of canned goods and kept three generators in his garage.

The problem was he hired my company to manage his investments, but because of his fear, he stepped on the brakes and told us to wait to get started. He didn't trust the government, but believed it was the government that would have to act to save us. He didn't trust the stock market. He thought it was both rigged and also the only way he could make money. He didn't trust the global economy. He thought the Chinese were going to take over the world while at the same time he believed that America would continue to be the dominant world power. It was very difficult to get him to commit to anything. He agreed he needed financial advice but was tentative in receiving it. Cognitive dissonance owned him.

When people are stuck and refuse to act, all you can do is go to work on the relationship and get small agreements. Small agreements will eventually lead to big ones. Arguing with people that their point of view is wrong is a surefire way to push them away. I made sure I continued to build rapport, listen carefully, acknowledge his needs and ask lots of questions to get him to challenge his own thinking. For example, saying, "If what you believe is true, having as much as you do in U.S. dollars is actually very risky." He said, "You're right."

Being patient with him also took a lot of self-control. However, because of the approach I took, he was willing to let me follow up with him monthly. After six months he finally decided to move forward. Some clients require more of your patience, persistence and tenacity.

The lesson is even when there is no perceived action happening, the decision to postpone action is an agreement (an agreement to postpone). When someone says, "I'm not moving forward," ask him if he's willing to talk about it for a few minutes. As long as you gain agreement to do so, you have an interim agreement.

Place Yourself on the Same Side of the Table

Can you really convince anyone of anything?

I used to believe I could. Arrogantly, I believed my logic, intellect, enthusiasm or sheer force would get my clients to give up their points of view and assume mine. However, in truth, I found it was a lot of effort and rarely worked. It would put me on the opposite side of an issue from them (something I'm not committed to) and often resulted in a "tug-of-war" or "push-me/pull-me" dynamic. It was adversarial and ineffective. Rather than choosing to collaborate, I chose to debate. Now I've come to see this as a major distraction and something that invalidated my clients' feelings. In essence, I was saying "Your point of view is wrong; my point of view is right."

If you "fight" someone and "win" you really lose. Winning a battle, proving you're right, for example, usually means losing the war and damaging the relationship. Exerting your expertise or knowledge over someone puts you in a superior position and the other person in an inferior one.

In the past, when a client shared his concerns with me, I tried to convince him he shouldn't be concerned. He'd voice a concern about the current administration in Washington D.C. and I told him, "Don't be." He'd voice a concern about terrorism and I said, "Don't be." Whatever opinion he expressed, I fell into the trap of taking the opposing point of view. This type of conversation centered around our contrary opinions versus his needs. As I discussed in Chapter Four, the problem with an opinion-based conversation is there is a winner and a loser. If you "convince" him to adopt your point of view you are the winner. That makes your client the loser (of his point of view).

Our points of view are wrapped up with our identities. To be successful in aligning with your clients, it's essential you're able to see multiple points of view. Rather than getting stuck on your opinion versus his, seek to explore his and find the need underneath the point of view. Needs-based conversations versus opinion-based conversations foster a win-win dynamic.

When you stop trying to convince your client to take your point of view, and simply put forth multiple points of view (demonstrating more than one possible future), it provides him the opportunity to choose the one he believes is best. You're supportive and collaborative rather than confrontational. If you find yourself battling or arguing with your client it's time to stop, collaborate and listen.

In 1969, country singer Ronny Light wrote the song "I'm a Lover (Not a Fighter)." I keep this title in mind when I find my clients are trying to battle with me. Two people can disagree without being disagreeable. They can fight for each other (together) instead of fighting with each other over their different points of view and work together toward the satisfaction of their mutual needs and wants.

We all like choices. We like to be in control of what we choose. In fact, when we feel we are coerced into a decision we generally come to resent it and/or the person who we feel coerced us. We like to choose freely and be satisfied with our choices.

Think about it from another perspective. How do you feel when you have very few (or only one) choice? Do you like to feel forced to take a certain action? Do you like it when someone's position is that you must adopt their way of thinking? The answer is likely no (and typically a strong no).

Instead of convincing, as in winning over, think of it as convincing with your client. Instead of trying to convince him of your company's or your specific point of view, enter his world view and discuss the views you share in common.

This doesn't mean you don't step in and correct a misperception or misunderstanding and say something like, "From my point of view that assumption is not correct," but that's very different from telling your client, "You're wrong." When you tell your client he is wrong, he's not going to like hearing that—no one likes to be wrong. However, when you tell him you've got a different take on his point of view or you think about it differently than he does, you bring him into a zone of collaborative conversation versus a combative conversation.

No one wins in a conversation that goes: "You're wrong." "No, you're wrong." "No, you're wrong." "No, you're wrong." But, like children, that's what's occurring in a conversation where both parties are holding on to their opinions and trying to convince the other of his point of view rather than both of them laying out their points of view side by side and seeing where they are aligned and discovering their differences. Alignment comes when you search deep enough (for example the need underneath the need underneath the need) and find fundamental human commonalities.

Searching for agreement is preferable to a make-wrong competition where you attempt to get your client to get off their position. You may have noticed when you're being stronger and more forceful than your clients in the attempt to get them to change their minds, the more likely they are to resist and persist in holding on to their position. This is the reason consultative conversations are superior to non-consultative, position-based convincing, persuading, cajoling or forcing models that are prevalently used.

Use Key Agreement Words

At some point in every conversation, you'll be asking your clients to agree to next steps. Be deliberate in how you do that. My recommendation is to use one of the five following words:

1. **Invite:** make a polite, formal, or friendly request to go somewhere or to do something.

2. **Request:** politely ask someone to do something.

3. **Suggest:** state or express indirectly, put forward, or offer something for consideration.

4. **Propose:** formally put forward an idea or plan for consideration, making an offer.

5. **Recommend:** advise or suggest a course of action.

Having these words ready for the asking and/or planning which one you're going to use will allow you to be powerful and clear.

Examples:

- "I invite you to consider taking the following action."
- "I request you think about this more."
- "I suggest we talk about this again in two weeks."
- "I propose you move forward soon."
- "I recommend we get started today."

Moreover, turning your agreement word into a noun from a verb might help you reduce perceived pressure. Instead of "I recommend you do _____", it's "My recommendation is that you do _____."

Examples:

- "Here's an invitation for you to consider."
- "I'd like to make a request of you."
- "My company has a suggestion for you."
- "I have a proposal for you."
- "We've got a recommendation ready for you."

Connecting your proposals directly to your client's needs makes them more powerful.

Examples:

- "Because you need long-term growth, I invite you to consider stocks."
- "I've heard you need time to think it over, I request you sleep on it and I'll call you tomorrow morning."
- "Here's a suggestion: due to your need to understand the plan in detail, why don't I put it in writing? You can take it home and read it over and then we can review it next week."
- "Given your need for financial security, I propose you begin setting aside three to six months emergency savings."
- "I understand you need clarity. My recommendation is you speak with your tax advisor and then we can circle back to discuss this next Wednesday."

- "I recommend you consolidate all of your accounts with us. You need simplicity at this stage of your life."

These are simple, but effective and constructive phrases to use. An important part of making an invitation, proposal, request, suggestion or recommendation is to avoid making how your client answers mean something about you. You have to depersonalize the answer in order to give him the opportunity to choose freely. When you get attached to a certain outcome, you'll limit your client's freedom to choose. He'll feel he has to say what you're hoping to hear versus knowing that he is free to make the decision that's best for himself.

Suggestions:

- Add a long pause after you make an invitation, request, suggestion, proposal or recommendation in order to make it very clear that you're asking for them to consider something.
- Be intentional about using a verb or a noun agreement word. Or, decide to use both in order that you can create some separation and then follow up with directness.
- Be committed to addressing and supporting the attainment of needs versus being attached to a certain outcome that you need to happen.

Clients will appreciate your commitment to supporting the attainment of their needs. This will make you more effective. The thoroughness with which you explored and addressed their needs will increase the likelihood that they'll say "yes."

Clients say "yes" when they see opportunity, potential and possibility. They say "yes" when there's some kind of catalyst that sparks them. They say "yes" when they are inspired. One of the conditions necessary for saying "yes" is mutual affinity and trust. Liking you and trusting you make it easier for them to say "yes."

Congruent, sincere and authentic invitations, proposals, requests, suggestions and recommendations create a new future for you and your relationship with your client. No matter how bleak or dark your future looks, you can return to the idea that anything is possible with a conversation for an invented or created future.

In order to know for sure if you're aligned and your client accepts your solution, you ask for a specific decision or action. If made properly, the client can comfortably say "yes" or "no." He may make it clear he's just not ready to agree to action. In that case, your question could be something like "Would you be willing to consider it?" or "Will you try it on for size?"

No matter how effective the conversation was up to the decision point, there's always a possibility of a hard "no." There are objections you just can't overcome no matter how effective, consultative, talented and convincing you are. Notwithstanding this truth, I believe there are things you can do to increase the likelihood that you will be effective in your conversations and that's the whole point of the book.

Getting to the final stage of a conversation and gaining agreement isn't something that comes easily or is always neat and tidy. The devil is in the details. Even if you had agreement in the first three parts of the conversation and you are in 98% agreement for action, things can easily slip away. Take the point of view it's not going to be neat and tidy. Conversations, like relationships, are hard work and sometimes messy. You may have heard the medical terminology of a productive cough. A cough is productive when you're able to bring up mucus (although it doesn't feel productive—it feels awful). In conversations, you may need to deal with the bad/tough stuff before you can breathe easily again.

You may even have to start over and create again, explore again and address again before you can resolve. Then and only then can you maximize the probability of gaining agreement for action. Persistence is required.

Conclusion

If you want to be successful in your role as a relationship manager, you'll always have to keep the next action in mind and pursue and negotiate agreement for action. For example, when will your client be speaking with you next? What is his agreed upon need and when will you follow up to see whether the solution you've provided, and he's agreed upon, is working for him? So long as your client has needs—which is always—you'll always have a job. Become skilled at gaining agreement and you'll have maximum impact in providing tangible value for your clients and your business.

One of the goals for a conversation is to be thought-provoking or feeling-provoking. If the final goal is to generate agreement for action, then the conversation needs to be a catalyst for new thoughts, new feelings and new actions. If a conversation doesn't provoke any new thoughts or new feelings, then what was the point of it? What is the point of a dialogue without a new result, where everything stays exactly the same, things don't progress and relationships don't deepen? The point is to create, generate, collaborate and celebrate the human experience.

Collaboration is key. Collaborate with your clients to discuss the solutions you can provide to meet their needs. A collaborative approach is more effective than trying to get your client to see things a certain way or coercing him into believing certain thoughts or taking certain actions.

Collaboration requires using everything I've discussed in this book. The optimal formula includes building rapport, using questions skillfully, listening, focusing on needs, exercising self-control, preparing and planning, creating, exploring, addressing and resolving.

My goal in this book was to teach you how to manage relationships one conversation at a time. To that end, I invite you to use the acronym CLEAR as a reminder of the model I've taught you.

1. Create the conversation: agree on the objectives and agenda.

2. Listen.

3. Explore to obtain a clear, complete and mutual understanding.

4. Address needs and objections by presenting solutions, matching features and handling/helping with objections.

5. Resolve and gain agreement for action.

The adjective "clear" means to understand something in a coherent, simple, straightforward way. If you're clear in your communications, you'll be much more effective.

If you don't have a specific method or approach to the management of your conversations and have just been "winging it," consider adopting the CLEAR formula. Even if you do have a solid approach, continue to refine and define what you're doing, and you'll experience newfound success in your life, your business and your relationships.

Conclusion

THANK YOU for reading *Conversations*. I'm grateful for the opportunity to share my ideas and experience with you.

- What will you do now that you've read the book?

- Do you plan to make changes in how you do things?

- Are you motivated to experiment and implement the strategies I've shared with you?

As far as next steps go, I have ten recommendations for you:

1. Commit to managing your relationships one conversation at a time.

2. Implement the ideas discussed in this book.

3. See your workplace as a conversation lab to experiment and practice.

4. Learn from your own and others' experience.

5. Raise your game to a new level by making incremental improvements to develop your skills.

6. Read books to feed your mind with new ideas that will make you better.

7. Take courses. (The two that made the most difference for me were The Dale Carnegie Course™ and The Landmark Forum®.)

8. Find a mentor or a coach.

9. Contact me to explore how I can be of service to you or your organization:

   Phone: 503-957-8500
   Email: ivan@conversations.biz
   Web: conversations.biz
   Social Media:
   - **Facebook.com/conversations.biz**
   - **Twitter @Ivan_Farber**
   - **LinkedIn**

10. Read the book again. (I've read it dozens of times as I've been writing and editing it and I learn or remember something important each and every time.)

Every conversation is an opportunity. Every conversation can be difference-making. As a relationship manager, the conversation is the arena in which you compete. Your success will be determined by how well you play the game of conversation. I invite you to play full out.

Make me proud.

Ten Lessons From 10,000 Conversations

Lesson 1. Build Rapport

The level of rapport impacts the effectiveness of every one of your conversations—it goes a long way toward determining their outcomes. Conversations are easier when rapport is present and are more difficult when rapport is missing.

Lesson 2. Use Questions Skillfully

Questions can be used to guide your conversations. They pave the path toward helping your clients understand their needs and discover ways to address them. But, to be effective using questions, you must use the right type of question at the right time.

Lesson 3. Listen

Listening is more important than talking. Listening is most impactful when it is done actively with intention and purpose. The better you listen, the better you'll be in creating powerful connections with your clients.

Lesson 4. Focus on Needs

Needs-based conversations result in positive outcomes. They help your clients see you as an ally and as someone who cares about them on a deeper level—beyond the normal expectations they have for a business relationship.

Lesson 5. Exercise Self-control

The reality is you can't control another person, you can only control yourself. Before you can competently manage a conversation, you must be disciplined and self-aware.

Lesson 6. Prepare and Plan

Conversations work better when you are prepared. When you have a plan and a structure to follow, you put yourself in a position to effectively manage and lead a conversation.

Lesson 7. Create

How a conversation starts matters. Engaging in a consultative needs-based conversation means discovering what your clients are seeking to accomplish and encouraging full participation.

Lesson 8. Explore

In order to get an understanding of your clients' needs beyond a superficial level, you must probe for understanding. The more depth you achieve, the stronger your relationships become.

Lesson 9. Address

Speak to your clients' needs and objections. Present ways to meet and satisfy their needs. Welcome their objections and take responsibility for helping to handle them.

Lesson 10. Resolve

Your goal is to problem solve and find solutions to satisfy your clients' needs. Then, you must gain agreement for action. The measure of a conversation is determined by the specific results it produces.

ABOUT THE AUTHOR

FOR THE PAST 25 YEARS, Ivan Farber has worked in marketing, sales, training and relationship management in the financial services industry. He's given hundreds of presentations to thousands of people. He currently works full time as a relationship manager at a privately held financial services company and maintains a coaching practice on the side. He was born and raised in Philadelphia. He obtained a B.A. in international relations from Tufts University and an M.B.A. in marketing from Boston College. He currently lives in Portland, Oregon with his wife Wendy and son Sam. He's a passionate Philadelphia Eagles fan and enthusiastic rider of his bicycle in all kinds of weather conditions.

"I have known Ivan for over 15 years and brought his ideas and coaching into several companies. If you need a coach that will help you improve yourself and take your game to the next level—look no further. He provides access to an abundance of ideas, wisdom and practical strategies that I use every day. He is the best coach I have ever worked with."

—Michael Van Sant, Wealth Advisor at Merriman, LLC

"Ivan has been an inspiration to me for many years. His infectious enthusiasm and belief in others has made him a trusted advisor to many including myself. His encouragement, pragmatism and energy always helped me reach new heights in my own endeavors. A genuine person, and a true professional—if he's on your team you're already ahead!"

—Jonathan Dalton, CEO and Co-Founder of THRIVE

"Ivan did an amazing job for our firm helping one of our top managers work with clients, potential clients and referral sources. He brings excellence and enthusiasm to his work. We give him the highest recommendation."

—Suzanne P. McGrath, President and Client Relationship Manager, Vision Capital Management, Inc.

"Ivan is a talented communicator, motivator and public speaker. He has successfully proven his worth as a resource. His greatest achievement lies in his ability to inspire others."

—Casey Roberts, Director of Sales, New England at Citizens Investment Services

"One of Ivan's strengths is his ability to build and maintain personal and working relationships. Ivan is always adding to the bottom line!"

—DW Johnson, Underwriter, Guild Mortgage Company

www.ingramcontent.com/pod-product-compliance
Lightning Source LLC
Chambersburg PA
CBHW060559200326
41521CB00007B/619